THE SAMURAI CAPTURE A KING

Okinawa 1609

STEPHEN TURNBULL

First published in 2009 by Osprey Publishing
Midland House, West Way, Botley, Oxford OX2 0PH, UK
443 Park Avenue South, New York, NY 10016, USA
E-mail: info@ospreypublishing.com

Print ISBN: 978 1 84603 442 8
PDF e-book ISBN: 978 1 84908 131 3

Page layout by: Bounford.com, Cambridge, UK
Index by Peter Finn
Typeset in Sabon
Maps by Bounford.com
Originated by PPS Grasmere Ltd, Leeds, UK
Printed in China through Worldprint

09 10 11 12 13   10 9 8 7 6 5 4 3 2 1

A CIP catalog record for this book is available from the British Library

FOR A CATALOGUE OF ALL BOOKS PUBLISHED BY OSPREY MILITARY AND AVIATION PLEASE CONTACT:

Osprey Direct, c/o Random House Distribution Center,
400 Hahn Road, Westminster, MD 21157
Email: uscustomerservice@ospreypublishing.com

Osprey Direct, The Book Service Ltd, Distribution Centre,
Colchester Road, Frating Green, Colchester, Essex, CO7 7DW
E-mail: customerservice@ospreypublishing.com

www.ospreypublishing.com

THE WOODLAND TRUST

Osprey Publishing are supporting the Woodland Trust, the UK's leading woodland conservation charity, by funding the dedication of trees.

ARTIST'S NOTE

Readers may care to note that the original paintings from which the colour plates of the figures, the ships and the battlescene in this book were prepared are available for private sale. All reproduction copyright whatsoever is retained by the Publishers. All enquiries should be addressed to:

Scorpio Gallery, PO Box 475, Hailsham, East Sussex, BN27 2SL, UK

The Publishers regret that they can enter into no correspondence upon this matter.

AUTHOR'S DEDICATION

To my two good friends and fellow scholars, Anthony Jenkins and Till Weber, without whose knowledge and support this book could not have been written.

AUTHOR'S ACKNOWLEDGEMENTS

I began working on this book in 2006, while attending the University of the Ryūkyūs as a Visiting Scholar. I was able to continue my research when I returned to Okinawa for a short period in 2008 (during my tenure as Visiting Professor of Japanese Studies at Akita International University). On this occasion, I retraced the course of the Okinawa raid by ship from Kagoshima via Amami-Oshima, landing on the Motobu peninsula in northern Okinawa where the Shimazu established their beachhead, and then travelled down the island to Shuri just as the Shimazu army had done. As a result of the two visits I was able to explore locations associated with the operation, including Naha Harbour, Shuri palace and the ancient Okinawan *gusuku*, sites from which resistance had been mounted against the invaders. However, the most important research materials I collected could only have been obtained through the kindness of several people who led me to the extensive, but very obscure, written primary sources. Here I thank in particular Professor Anthony Jenkins and Professor Till Weber of the University of the Ryūkyūs, together with the staff of Okinawa Prefectural Library, Okinawa Prefectural Museum and Kagoshima Prefectural Library. I was helped enormously in following up these leads, particularly in my search for illustrations, by Maiko Nishida of Akita International University, whose bibliographic skills led me to books that had long been forgotten. These included the only surviving complete set of *Ehon Ryūkyū Gunki* in Nara Prefectural Library, which I was kindly allowed to photograph. Some of the pictures appear here in a modern printed book for the first time.

EDITOR'S NOTE

A full glossary to the Japanese terms used in this book can be found on pages 60–61.

Dates of days and months are given first in the lunar calendar, then according to the Gregorian calendar.

Unless indicated otherwise, all the photographs in this volume are from the author's own collection.

NAMING CONVENTIONS

Japanese names are written with the family name first. In the case of names of islands, the suffixes -shima, -jima and -tō, all of which mean 'island', have been retained within the romanised names for clarity, as has the suffix -mon, meaning 'gateway'.

CONTENTS

INTRODUCTION

Four hundred years ago the independent kingdom of Ryūkyū, the group of islands which now form the Japanese prefecture of Okinawa, was subjected to a rapid, fierce and brilliantly executed raid by the army of its nearest neighbour, Shimazu Iehisa, the *daimyo* of the province of Satsuma. The operation resulted in the capture of the king of Ryūkyū and the annexation of his kingdom by Satsuma, a situation that was maintained for two and a half centuries until the creation of modern Japan. In brief, the military operation comprised of a series of armed landings along the chain of islands leading to Okinawa, the establishment of a secure beachhead, and then a two-pronged advance by land and sea against Okinawa's main harbour of Naha and the royal palace at Shuri. Within a matter of days the king of Ryūkyū was a prisoner, and 250 years of Satsuma control had begun.

The period in which this audacious raid was carried out is significant as it took place six years after the establishment of the Tokugawa shogunate, and was therefore conducted during a time of peace. In 1600, Tokugawa Ieyasu had triumphed at the decisive battle of Sekigahara, following which he then re-established the post of *shogun* in the name of his family, a position that was maintained until 1868. By 1609, the Tokugawa control of Japan was virtually complete, and only two serious rebellions were to challenge their supremacy during the next two and a half centuries. The first came in 1614, when the Tokugawa family were forced to conduct the great siege of Osaka Castle, where tens of thousands of disaffected samurai sought to challenge the new dictatorship. The Osaka campaign ended with a Tokugawa victory, as did the much smaller-scale Shimabara Rebellion (an uprising largely involving Japanese peasants) in 1638. Yet while both these events directly challenged the rule of the Tokugawa and proved unwelcome reminders of the former time of civil war, the Okinawa raid in 1609 was different. It was an operation conducted with the *shogun*'s blessing against an independent neighbouring kingdom. The only event with any parallel to this had been Japan's single other contemporary overseas expedition, the unsuccessful invasion of Korea in 1592. The great contrast between the two concerns the outcomes. Whereas Korea had been a failure, Okinawa was not only a dramatic success, it was also a unique event in Japanese history. Throughout the whole samurai era, it proved to be the only successful act of aggression against a sovereign state.

The Okinawa raid of 1609 was carried out both willingly and eagerly on the *shogunate*'s behalf by the *daimyo* of Satsuma, Shimazu Iehisa, whose family had maintained a legal claim to the Ryūkyū archipelago for many centuries. Despite being on the losing side at Sekigahara and having to flee ignominiously from the battlefield, the *shogun* treated the Shimazu family differently to almost every other *daimyo* in Japan, whether friend or foe. Not for the first time in Japanese history, the victor (who had defeated the geographically distant Shimazu) foresaw both the difficulties of mounting a long-range expedition to crush them and the advantages of leaving them to rule the remote but strategic area of Japan that they knew so well. The Shimazu were therefore excluded from the massive programme of transfer of territories, whereby almost all the other *daimyo* were moved about at will. The loyal *fudai daimyo* were given fiefs where they could control the *tozama daimyo* who had been allowed to survive after opposing the Tokugawa at Sekigahara. Exceptionally, the *tozama* Shimazu were allowed to stay on what had been their homeland for centuries, and, even more remarkably, were then invited to go to war again.

The well-executed Okinawa raid is a fascinating snapshot of samurai warfare at its peak. Toyotomi Hideyoshi's invasion of Korea in 1592 had shown how large numbers of troops could be conveyed overseas to carry out a lightning attack using massed firearms, arson and terror – tactics that were to be displayed at a micro-level on Okinawa. All the familiar aspects of samurai organisation, arms and armour, strategy and tactics were brilliantly displayed in this operation. Although five years later European cannon would be brought to bear against the huge fortress of Osaka in a prolonged siege, the Okinawa raid demonstrated the characteristics of rapid movement, drawing from experiences of an earlier age and more than a century of civil war.

Given that this was a unique and dramatic operation, it is surprising to note that the Okinawa invasion is virtually unknown outside Japan. It is mentioned briefly in several standard histories of the country written in English, but only one academic article in a European language has ever been published about the attack itself. Even though the raid was executed between two of the most famous campaigns in Japanese history, Sekigahara and Osaka, the events of Okinawa remain a footnote to the early accounts of the Tokugawa Period, which focused more heavily on internal control than on overseas adventures. Okinawa has therefore become Japan's forgotten war. It was the final attempt to create an overseas empire before Japan shut itself off from the outside world in 1639, bringing almost all overseas trade and foreign warfare to an end. From 1639 onwards, Japan's overseas contacts were limited to China, Korea and a tiny Dutch settlement at Dejima in Nagasaki Bay. The events of Okinawa in 1609 were to remain in folk memory as Japan's last foreign war until modern times.

Shimazu Iehisa, *daimyo* (feudal lord) of Satsuma, in whose name the Okinawa raid was carried out. Iehisa became *daimyo* of Satsuma following the family's involvement on the losing side at the Battle of Sekigahara in 1600. The Okinawa operation represented his submission to the Tokugawa in addition to resolving a centuries-old claim to Ryūkyū (Okinawa).

ORIGINS

Ryūkyū and Okinawa

Modern Japan consists of four main islands and hundreds of smaller ones. The large islands are: Hokkaidō in the north; the main island of Honshū, where lie the ancient and modern capitals of Kyoto and Tokyo; Shikoku, which nestles next to Honshū beside the Inland Sea; and Kyūshū, the great southern island that was for centuries the main gateway for trade and cultural contact between Japan and foreign nations. From the southernmost tip of Kyūshū, a long chain of islands stretches across the ocean to a point just over 100 miles from Taiwan. Administratively, these smaller islands belong to the prefectures of either Okinawa or Kagoshima, the ancient domain of the Shimazu family in southern Kyūshū. A glance at a modern map of Japan shows that the border between the two prefectures lies in the sea between the main island of Okinawa and the Amami Islands, but centuries ago matters were not so exact. Then, any such 'borderline' would have been an interface between two different sovereign states. A long argument over where that line should be drawn exercised the minds of the kings of Ryūkyū and the *daimyo* of Satsuma for many centuries, which eventually led to the bloody climax in 1609.

The political complexity behind the 1609 operation is reflected in the choice of names applied to the collection of islands that became the Shimazu's target. Ryūkyū is sometimes used as a geographical term to denote the entire island chain running between Kagoshima and Taiwan. However, when used in a political sense it refers to the kingdom that existed there until 1879, one that did not rule over the whole archipelago and one that also lost a number of its northern islands after 1609. The kingdom of Ryūkyū, which was controlled by Satsuma from 1609 onwards, lasted until 1879 when it was absorbed by Japan and renamed 'Oki-nawa' (from its resemblance to a length of rope tossed carelessly into the sea). Modern Okinawa prefecture comprises 55 islands, but the name Okinawa is also used to identify the main island of the group. Following the terrible battle of Okinawa in 1945, the American occupation resurrected the name Ryūkyū but in adding an '-s', referred to the region as 'the Ryūkyūs'. When the prefecture reverted to Japan in 1972, the name Okinawa

The busy streets of the town that surrounded the palace of Shuri, depicted here in imaginative detail by the artist Okada Gyōkuzan (1737–1812) in *Ehon Ryūkyū Gunki*, an illustrated historical romance based on the story of the Okinawa raid of 1609.

was re-adopted. As a further confusion, European visitors to Ryūkyū in the 18th and 19th centuries often wrote its name as 'Loochoo'. For clarity in the book, the term 'Ryūkyū' is used in a historical context and 'Okinawa' for the geographical location of an event.

The first mention of Ryūkyū in Japanese history occurs in 1187 when reference is made to the accession to the throne of Shunten, a figure said to be the son of the exiled Minamoto Tametomo. A great samurai archer, Tametomo (1139–1170) became the hero of a brief conflict in Kyoto in 1156 known as the Hōgen Incident. Following the defeat of his political faction, Tametomo was exiled. A story is told that on seeing a boatload of samurai coming to kill him, Tametomo fired an arrow and sank their vessel, whereupon he retired and committed *seppuku*. However, an alternative legend has him escape to distant Okinawa, where he became the ancestor of the kings of Ryūkyū.

The political context of the Tametomo legend links the founding of the royal house of Ryūkyū directly to Japan, making the assertion that the islands had always been an integral part of the Japanese empire. This was a belief deeply held by rulers of the neighbouring Satsuma province, who maintained a long-standing claim to the whole Ryūkyū archipelago, dating from the time of Shimazu Tadahisa. In 1186 the first *shogun*, Minamoto Yoritomo, granted the governorship of Satsuma to his illegitimate son, Tadahisa. This had been a deliberate act on Yoritomo's part because Satsuma was as far away from the capital at Kamakura, and the hostility of his wife towards his son, as was geographically possible. Its remote location allowed Tadahisa's descendants to enjoy many centuries of unchallenged rule in Japan's southern corner. Their first formal claim on Ryūkyū dates from 1206, when Shimazu Tadahisa is supposed to have been granted the additional title of 'Lord of the Twelve Southern Islands', an imprecise term referring to Ryūkyū.

The *shogun* Minamoto Yoritomo was the nephew of the late Tametomo, but the supposition that the kings of Ryūkyū were descended from Shimazu Tadahisa's great-uncle did not impress the actual rulers of the island kingdom. Even the legal basis of Tadahisa's appointment in 1206 as overlord of Ryūkyū could be challenged, because it was based on a written document that the Shimazu later maintained was lost in a fire. Yet based on these two elements of shaky evidence, the lords of Satsuma frequently made claims of ownership to Ryūkyū during the ensuing centuries, causing several diplomatic problems. A document dated 1441 referred to the three provinces of Satsuma, Hyūga and Osumi on the island of Kyūshū and confirmed them to be under the governorship of the Shimazu, the family also being known as '*Ryūkyū no shugo*' (governors of Ryūkyū). These claims were to be incorporated into the surrender document that was signed after the 1609 raid with the words: 'The islands of Ryūkyū have from ancient times been a feudal dependency of Satsuma.'

Rivalry for Ryūkyū

Although the 1609 raid may have been launched from Satsuma against Ryūkyū, such expansionist moves had never been one-sided. In fact over previous centuries, the Ryūkyūans had shown themselves to be the more aggressive rival of the two. Ryūkyūan expansion had begun with the islands near to Okinawa, and the neighbouring islands of Iheya and the Kerama group came under Ryūkyūan control in 1264. This had all been carried out against a background of considerable conflict within the large island now known as Okinawa. For over a century (1314–1429), the control of Okinawa had been fiercely contested by the three rival 'principalities' of Hokuzan (north), Chūzan (central) and Nanzan (south). The term 'principality' is

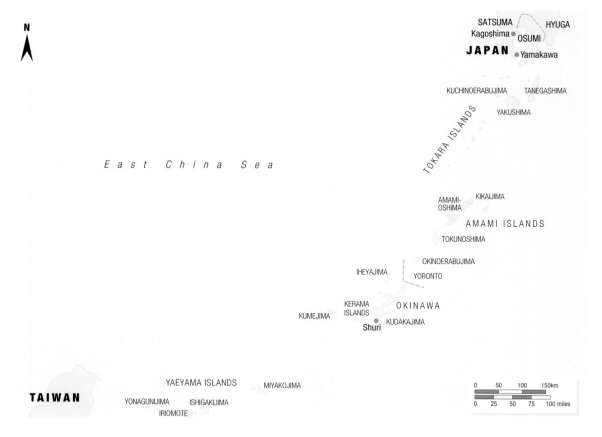

SATSUMA HYUGA
Kagoshima OSUMI
JAPAN Yamakawa

KUCHINOERABUJIMA TANEGASHIMA

YAKUSHIMA

TOKARA ISLANDS

East China Sea

AMAMI- KIKAIJIMA
OSHIMA

AMAMI ISLANDS

TOKUNOSHIMA

OKINOERABUJIMA

IHEYAJIMA YORONTO

KERAMA OKINAWA
ISLANDS
KUMEJIMA KUDAKAJIMA
Shuri

YAEYAMA ISLANDS MIYAKOJIMA

TAIWAN YONAGUNIJIMA ISHIGAKIJIMA
IRIOMOTE

0 50 100 150km
0 25 50 75 100 miles

The island chain between
Japan and China.

used as a linguistic convenience rather than a precise political definition. Their rulers
were normally referred to as kings, while lesser warlords, and rulers from an earlier
period, were called *aji*.

In 1406, a warlord called Shō Hashi deposed the ruler of Chūzan and replaced
him with his own father Shō Shishō. After a considerable military campaign, Shō
Hashi united the three rival principalities in 1429 to create the kingdom of Ryūkyū,
which proceeded to rule over the whole of Okinawa Island. The new military strength
on Okinawa meant that the conquest of the more distant Miyakojima and the
Yaeyama group (which lay 176 and 262 miles to the south respectively) could now
be contemplated, and both objectives were eventually achieved. Miyakojima was
annexed in 1500, while the conquest of the Yaeyama Islands, which included Ishigaki,
Iriomote and Yonaguni, took place in 1509 after a campaign involving 3,000 men on
46 ships. This extended Ryūkyūan influence to the very edge of the archipelago. The
ruler of Kumejima, an island to the west of Okinawa, succumbed in 1507.

In spite of their ancestral claims to the whole of Ryūkyū, the Shimazu family of
Satsuma made no attempt to interfere with the offensives made by the Ryūkyūan
kings to the south and west of Okinawa. What brought Ryūkyū and Satsuma into
collision were the expansionist activities of successive kings, aimed in a northerly
direction against the Amami Islands (Oshima, Kikaijima, Tokunoshima,
Okinoerabujima and Yorontō). These were regarded as acts of aggression that pushed
Ryūkyūan affairs well within the Satsuma realm of interest. Oshima, the largest of
the Amami Islands, which lies just under halfway to Satsuma at a point about 220
miles from Naha, eventually fell to an attack by the kingdom of Ryūkyū in about

1440. Yet this did not give Ryūkyū complete control of the archipelago, because the fighting continued for several years. This ongoing border dispute between Ryūkyū and Satsuma is confirmed in a comment contained within a Korean document called *Joseon Wangjo Sillok*, a travelogue compiled in 1453 by the Korean survivors of a shipwreck. It relates how a 'disastrous wind' had arisen to cast them ashore on the tiny uninhabited island of Gajashima, which lies within the Tokara group about midway between Amami-Oshima and the Satsuma mainland. The Koreans recorded vaguely that Gajashima belonged to both Ryūkyū and Satsuma, perhaps indicating they had been washed up on the front line of a continuing quarrel. The Korean survivors were eventually transported to the island of Okinawa itself. Here, they visited Shuri Castle, the stronghold of the king of Ryūkyū, and had the opportunity to observe the military prowess of their hosts in matters such as firearms. They also learned that Kikaijima, another island of the Amami group, was still disputed territory some ten years after the conquest of Oshima.

Long after the Korean visitors had departed, Kikaijima's continued resistance prompted the personal intervention of King Shō Toku, who attacked the island in 1466 with 2,000 men on 50 ships. Shō Toku was one of Ryūkyū's great warrior kings, and is portrayed in history as a headstrong youth imbued with romantic ideas of the *wakō* pirates who made use of Ryūkyū for their own raids. Shō Toku adopted as his crest the 'three comma-shaped jewels in a circle' device of Hachiman, the god of war, that was used by the pirates and later became the flag of the Ryūkyū kings. Although Shō Toku's expedition continued the expansion of Ryūkyūan interests, Kikaijima provided no new resources or important harbour. It eventually proved to be such a strain on the treasury that Shō Toku was deposed while he was away 'dallying' with the chief priestess of Kudaka Island, a breach of royal etiquette that would have enraged his courtiers as much as his failure to exploit the conquest of Kikaijima.

From the 1440s onwards, the Ryūkyūan kings stubbornly defended their occupation of the Amami Islands against any attempt by Satsuma to recapture them. After fierce fighting, they drove off an expedition mounted by the Shimazu against Oshima in 1493, while rebels on Oshima, who objected to Ryūkyūan rule, prompted an armed intervention in 1537 by King Shō Shin. It is thought that in 1571, a similar expedition was carried out against rebels by King Shō Gen, which would have been the last aggressive move by Ryūkyū to the north before 1609.

The Shimazu family of Satsuma were not the only *daimyo* to have had designs on Ryūkyū in the years leading to 1609, and trade interests with China through Ryūkyū undoubtedly had an influence on this. The names of Ouchi, Hosokawa and Otomo are mentioned in terms of coveting Ryūkyūan territory, but only two *daimyo* ever threatened to challenge the Shimazu's long-standing claim. The first was Kamei

A view of the volcano of Sakurajima which lies in the bay off Kagoshima. The photograph is taken from the site of Tsurumaru castle, the seat of the Shimazu *daimyo*.

Korenori (1557–1612), who had served Toyotomi Hideyoshi in the 1582 expedition to crush the Mōri family. This important campaign had been hastily concluded when Hideyoshi received news of the death of his master Oda Nobunaga. Later that year, Hideyoshi's subsequent triumph at the battle of Yamazaki set him on the path towards becoming the ruler of all Japan, so generous rewards were in order for those who had helped him. Kamei Korenori asked Hideyoshi for Izumo province, which would have provided him with an ideal base to develop foreign trade, but when Hideyoshi informed him that Izumo was being given to the Mōri as part of their overall surrender agreement, Korenori suggested Ryūkyū as an alternative. The idea pleased Hideyoshi, who realised that this would give him an ally on the way to China as well as outflank the Shimazu, who had yet to submit to Hideyoshi's authority. He therefore presented Korenori with his own war fan, and wrote upon it the date, his name 'Toyotomi Hideyoshi' and the coveted title 'Kamei Ryūkyū no kami' (Lord Kamei of Ryūkyū).

Not surprisingly, news that their ancestral claim had been casually passed to another was not received well in Satsuma, so the Shimazu asked Hosokawa Yūsai and Ishida Mitsunari (senior government administrators) to remind Hideyoshi of the Shimazu's long relationship with the islands. Kamei Korenori was not deterred, and in 1591 he sailed to claim his prize, only to find his fleet intercepted by the Shimazu. At that time, Hideyoshi was busy preparing for the invasion of Korea so took little notice of a minor dispute among his followers. Korenori quickly abandoned his plans, and very soon both the Shimazu and Kamei samurai were fighting side by side on the Korean peninsula. Korenori kept the war fan, and it entered the story once again when, just a few years later, it featured as part of the booty acquired by the Koreans after the Japanese defeat at the naval battle of Dangpo. Its description, together with the inscription on it referring to the Ryūkyūs, was faithfully recorded by the Korean Admiral Yi Sun-sin.

A further attempt to seize Ryūkyū was made by Ukita Hideie. He was one of the defeated commanders at Sekigahara, and sought sanctuary after the battle with the sympathetic Shimazu of Satsuma. Hideie, however, planned to create a new territory for himself among the Ryūkyū Islands, in spite of strict orders from Shimazu Iehisa, the current *daimyo*, not to do anything of the sort. The Ukita fleet haughtily set sail from the Tokara Islands but was then wrecked by a typhoon. Not long afterwards, the Shimazu punished him for his presumption by handing him over to the Tokugawa, and Ukita Hideie ended his days in 1662 on the island of Hachijōjima, far from Ryūkyū, as an exile, not as a *daimyo*.

The Shimazu *Daimyo*

The 1609 expedition was carried out by the family that had shown themselves to be the great survivors of Medieval Japan, both in war and in peace. With the triumph of the Tokugawa and the re-establishment of the shogunate in 1603, a century and a half of civil war had effectively come to an end. This long period of unrest, known as the *Sengoku jidai*, can be likened to a similar period of conflict in ancient China. It is thought to have started with the Onin War of 1467, when a succession dispute within the shogunate exposed the weaknesses of that long-standing institution. The most important result of the upheaval, which caused extensive damage within Kyoto itself, was that local warlords began to assert themselves as petty kings, knowing that the central authority lacked the power to control them. Some of these new *daimyo*, 'great names' as they termed themselves, had formerly ruled their provinces on the *shogun*'s behalf as his *shugo*. Now they created territories of their own and defended them with armies of samurai. Other *daimyo* were simply opportunists with military skills, but the overall result was to temporarily redraw the map of Japan until reunification could be achieved.

For the Shimazu family the transition from the post of governor, granted to their ancestor Shimazu Tadahisa, to that of ruling *daimyo* of Satsuma, was brought about largely by Shimazu Takahisa (1514–1571). The move was a very smooth one, untroubled by serious local opposition and carried out at a very great distance from Kyoto. Yet Satsuma was by no means a cultural backwater. In fact two of the most significant developments in Japanese history occurred on Shimazu territory. The first was brought about by a shipwreck in 1543, when a group of Portuguese traders, carrying with them the first European-style firearms ever seen in Japan, landed on the island of Tanegashima. Takahisa immediately realised the potential of these new weapons and authorised their production within his territory, a decision that marked the beginning of Japan's military revolution. Six years later, St Francis Xavier brought Christianity to Japan when he landed in Satsuma, and for a few years at least, Satsuma became Japan's gateway to Europe.

With firearms to hand, Shimazu Takahisa faced up to the challenges posed by the breakdown of the *shogun*'s authority, and used them to his family's advantage in a programme of conquest that eventually resulted in the Shimazu becoming rulers of almost all of Kyūshū. They began by reinforcing their control over the three provinces of Satsuma, Osumi and Hyūga, that they had nominally ruled since the days of the Minamoto. Of the three, only Satsuma was truly theirs. Deploying firearms in anger for the first time, the Shimazu asserted their authority over Osumi and Hyūga in a series of battles. Following Takahisa's death in 1571, the work of developing the family's dominion was carried on by his four sons, Yoshihisa, Yoshihiro, Toshihisa and Iehisa. The eldest, Yoshihisa (1533–1611), took the Shimazu to the peak of their ascendancy. In 1578, when Otomo Sōrin of Bungo province invaded Hyūga, the Shimazu responded by destroying the Otomo's expeditionary army at the battle of Mimigawa. Then in 1584, they marched north from Satsuma and defeated the Ryūzōji at the battle of Okita-Nawate on the Shimabara peninsula. A year later, they were making plans for the conquest of the Otomo's home province, which would then make them masters of the whole of Kyūshū. This prospect, however, prompted the intervention of Toyotomi Hideyoshi, whose vast programme for the reunification of Japan would not be thwarted by ancient rulers such as the Shimazu. In 1587, Hideyoshi launched the invasion of Kyūshū in the guise of helping the Otomo. It was the largest military operation ever conducted in Japan up to that time, and drove the Shimazu back into Satsuma province from whence they had come. Hideyoshi had no desire to annihilate the Shimazu, merely to bring them under his control and then use their enormous local influence to rule their remote provinces on his behalf. As part of the peace settlement, Shimazu Yoshihisa was required to cede his domains to his brother Yoshihiro (1535–1619).

By 1591, Hideyoshi had received submission from every *daimyo* in Japan, and in an act of megalomania, decided to conquer China as well. The Korean peninsula provided the easiest route towards Beijing, but its

The *daimyo* of Satsuma, Shimazu Iehisa, bids farewell to his fleet as it sails from Yamakawa Harbour for Okinawa. This picture is interesting because it is a re-working by the artist Okada Gyokuzan of a scene used in his previous book *Ehon Taikō-ki* which shows Hideyoshi bidding farewell to the Japanese fleet as it sails for Korea. The heraldry on the sails of the ships has been changed, as has the general's flag. (Illustration taken from *Ehon Ryūkyū Gunki* – ERG)

A distant view of the castle of Shuri, within whose walls rise the roofs of the royal palace of the kings of Ryūkyū. We are looking across the artificial lake of Ryutan, created in 1427.

inhabitants had no intention of letting Hideyoshi's army have an uninterrupted journey, and a savage and disastrous war began in 1592. Shimazu Yoshihiro led the Satsuma contingent in the invasion, which was masterminded by Toyotomi Hideyoshi. Unfortunately, Hideyoshi was ignorant of the geographical and political realities of the relationships between Japan, Korea and Ming China. His lack of knowledge also extended to any real understanding of the history between Satsuma and Ryūkyū, because in 1590 Hideyoshi told King Shō Nei of Ryūkyū that he would be expected to provide troops for the invasion while the retired *daimyo*, Shimazu Yoshihisa, would oversee the arrangements. Yoshihisa, who did not want to see an armed force raised on Okinawa, suggested to Hideyoshi that the Ryūkyūan contribution should be made in terms of gold, silver and grain instead. This was agreed, but no shipment was made until the Shimazu put pressure upon Shō Nei, and even then only a token contribution was forthcoming. Hideyoshi had also been concerned that Ryūkyū, which conducted active trade with Ming China, might alert the Chinese to his plans, so he ordered King Shō Nei to break off all trade relations immediately. The king refused and instead reported the invasion plans to a group of Chinese envoys, urging them to inform their emperor. This was a great embarrassment to the Shimazu; Hideyoshi believed they exerted considerable influence over the islands, but the king's defiance had now exposed their actual lack of control. Fortunately Hideyoshi was too preoccupied with his invasion plans to notice such small details, and once in Korea, the Shimazu served Hideyoshi loyally and well, particularly during the last days of the Japanese withdrawal in 1598, when Shimazu Yoshihiro and his son Tadatsune withstood a massive Chinese attack on the fortress of Sacheon.

Toyotomi Hideyoshi died in 1598, leaving a power vacuum around his infant son Hideyori. Matters were resolved at the decisive battle of Sekigahara in 1600 when the Tokugawa defeated a loose coalition of other *daimyo*, among whom the Shimazu fought. Yoshihiro conducted himself with great bravery and as the battle finished, he fought his way out of encirclement and began a long and humiliating journey back to Satsuma, only to suffer the indignity of being imprisoned by his retired elder brother. The Shimazu had survived defeat for a second time, but once again it cost them a change of leadership. Yoshihiro was forced to retire and pass the territory to his son Tadatsune, who formally submitted to the Tokugawa in 1602. Tokugawa Ieyasu, who was shortly to acquire the title of *shogun*, treated the new Shimazu *daimyo* with respect and authorised Tadatsune to take the ancient Tokugawa surname of Matsudaira. He also bestowed upon Tadatsune one of the syllables from his own name. For some reason, Tadatsune decided to change his name completely to Iehisa, the name of one of his illustrious uncles who had died in 1587. Shimazu Iehisa, therefore, was the *daimyo* of Satsuma when his family carried out their 1609 raid.

The raid of 1609 represented an important policy shift by the Shimazu. In spite of their long-standing claim on Ryūkyū, they had been too busy acquiring, defending and then losing territory on Kyūshū during the latter part of the 16th century, to make their theoretical assertion a reality. Now, once the dust had settled after Sekigahara, the Shimazu's newly- established and cordial relationship with the new *shogun* made such an expedition attractive to both parties. In addition to giving Shimazu Iehisa a new name, Tokugawa Ieyasu had also confirmed on him the ancient Shimazu title of 'Lord of the Twelve Islands'. However, his own political horizon stretched much wider. Having learned of the Spanish seizure of the Philippines in 1571, and seen Spanish presence in Japan established through Christian missionaries, Ieyasu greatly feared Spain's influence. A way of frustrating any potential move by Spain against Japan in the future would be to strengthen Japanese influence along the chain of islands through which a European force would have to pass, so an envoy was sent to Okinawa requiring the King of Ryūkyū to submit to the rule of the Tokugawa, just as every other *daimyo* in Japan had done. The king treated the demand with as much contempt as he had dealt with the earlier request to supply troops for the Japanese invasion of Korea. Faced with such defiance, Tokugawa Ieyasu willingly granted Shimazu Iehisa's request to chastise the Ryūkyūans for their presumption, and from that moment on, the prospect of a military move against Okinawa began to acquire real likelihood.

Shimazu Iehisa's primary goal was probably the simple one of regaining the Amami Islands. A plan for such an expedition was drawn up in 1606 and funded by an allocation of silver, but the scheme was abandoned even before the necessary warships were built. It was, however, at the renewed prompting of Iehisa's new master in Edo, Tokugawa Hidetada, who had succeeded his retired father, that a workable invasion plan was finally put on the table in 1608. This time, the aims went far beyond the simple recovery of the Amami Islands – the whole Ryūkyū Kingdom was now the target. Hoping that the matter could be settled by negotiation, in the eighth lunar month of Keichō 13 (1608), Shimazu Iehisa sent three senior retainers, Ichiki Obusei, Murao Shōsei and the priest Daijiji Seiin Osho as envoys to Ryūkyū, to present Satsuma's demands to the king. The Ryūkyūans were reminded of the debt they owed to Satsuma, dating back to the time of Hideyoshi's Korean invasion. It was spelt out in grandiose terms how they had been spared from making a military contribution through the generosity of the family who had been their real overlords since 1206. As well as this, they were told they should pay homage to the Tokugawa and, at the very least, to cede the Amami Islands to Satsuma. When these demands were refused, the *shogun* officially commanded Shimazu Iehisa to pacify Ryūkyū on the 19th day of the ninth lunar month (from now on to be written in the style 9m 19d) of that same year, which, when converted to the Gregorian calendar, was 27 October 1608.

11 MARCH 1609

Satsuma army begins gathering at Yamakawa

In this painted screen in the Reimeikan Museum in Kagoshima we see the Shimazu army in action during the Battle of Sekigahara. Very similar flags bearing the *mon* of a cross in a ring would have been seen on Okinawa in 1609.

INITIAL STRATEGY

Sources for the Raid

As the events of 1609 are so little known outside Japan, there are few written accounts in English apart from short passages in George H. Kerr's *Okinawa: The History of an Island People* and A. L. Sadler's *The Maker of Modern Japan*. The literature about Satsuma's occupation of Ryūkyū is more comprehensive, but no book or article contains more than a brief mention of the war through which it all began, and only one academic article on the subject has ever been published in any European language. This is 'Die Ryukyu Expedition Unter Shimazu Iehisa' by R. Binkenstein, which was published in an early issue of *Monumenta Nipponica* in 1941. Binkenstein, however, made no use of the primary sources referred to below. His sources were largely confined to *gunkimono* style accounts of the campaign, where the exploits of the brave Shimazu samurai were blatantly exaggerated for the benefit of their descendants, similar to the famous medieval *gunkimono* such as *Heike Monogatari* and *Taiheiki*. Recognising these limitations, Binkenstein included little discussion of the invasion itself and concentrated instead on the events leading up to it.

The authentic written sources for the Okinawa expedition are few in number and very obscure. They are however very reliable, and may be divided into three categories. The most important are three eyewitness accounts of the events. The first, from the Ryūkyūan perspective, is *Kyan Nikki*, which was compiled in about 1627 by the priest Kyan Ueekata (Kian Oyakata) who, originally from Sakai in Izumi province, went to Okinawa in 1600 and became a close associate of King Shō Nei. In *Kyan Nikki*, almost the entire invasion is described in detail by a man who had been involved in the earlier negotiations to avoid the war, saw it unfold on Okinawa and then accompanied his king into exile.

The other two eyewitness sources are from the Satsuma standpoint and are included in a published collection of historical documents from Kagoshima prefecture. One is entitled *Ryūkyū Tokai Nichi Ki* and is the diary of Ichiki Magobe'e Iemoto, who served in the invading Shimazu army in the Takayama *shū* (Takayama Company – named after the place in which the unit was stationed). Ichiki was involved in the section of the army that took the overland route after landing on Okinawa. The other account, *Ryūkyū Gunki*, was written by an eyewitness who sailed with the fleet as it attempted to force an entry into Naha Harbour. The author is believed to have been a *funegashira* (ship's captain) based on the Tokara Islands. Only seven out of the twelve Tokara Islands are inhabited, hence the expression *Shichitō* (Seven Islands) that is used in his account. Despite its title, *Ryūkyū Gunki* is not a romantic *gunkimono* but a sober and often brutal account of the invasion in which no attempt is made to disguise the various setbacks experienced by the Satsuma army. Using these three primary sources, it is possible to recreate a day-to-day account of the operation from three different locations and from two different perspectives.

The Shimazu family archives are the second valuable source of authentic written material, containing documents relating to the planning, organisation and execution of the raid, such as muster lists, notes on casualties and official reports.

The third category comprises two *gunkimono*, the *Shimazu Ryūkyū Gunseiki* of 1663 and *Satsuryū Gundan*, which is an abridgement of the former. *Shimazu Ryūkyū Gunseiki* is a fictionalised account of the conflict in which the Shimazu family of the latter half of the 17th century could read of the exploits of their fathers in the family's last great expedition. As already mentioned, embellishments and exaggerations are common in *gunkimono*, particularly with regard to troop numbers, but the most curious aspect of *Shimazu Ryūkyū Gunseiki* is that all the names of the generals who took part and the battles in which they fought have been changed. The actual commanding officer, a samurai general called Kabayama Hisataka, is never mentioned; instead the leadership of the army is credited to the veteran Shimazu retainer Niiro Musashi-no-kami, who did not actually take part in the invasion. At the time of the raid he was already 84 years old, and he died just a year later in 1610. Similarly there is no sense of geography, so the attack on Yōkeidan Castle – described as the way in to Ryūkyū – may actually refer to the Shimazu's initial attack on the fortress of Nakijin, or it may be an entirely fictional episode. *Shimazu Ryūkyū Gunseiki* is nonetheless very revealing about the attitudes of the samurai class at that time. According to *Shimazu Ryūkyū Gunseiki*, bullets always 'fly like rain' and war cries invariably 'shake heaven and earth', while the Shimazu force is sometimes referred to as the 'Japanese army' and Japan as 'the land of the gods'. Despite their many elaborations, the *gunkimono* may also contain some hints about the way the army was organised. During the early 19th century an illustrated account of the raid was produced. Entitled *Ehon Ryūkyū Gunki* (ERG), it contains a narrative based on *Shimazu Ryūkyū Gunseiki*.

Army Leadership

Shimazu Iehisa, the *daimyo* of Satsuma, played no part in the actual military operation, although this decision was not based on any lack of soldierly skill. In 1598, he and his father had become the heroes of the battle of Sacheon, and his subsequent rule of Satsuma had shown that he had the necessary qualities of ruthlessness and tenacity to carry out such an audacious operation. The following year, Iehisa's mansion had become the setting for the murder of Ijuin Tadamune, a man who had once been one of the Shimazu's most loyal retainers. Tadamune's personal ambitions and wealth, arising from his service in Korea, had tempted him into setting up a petty kingdom of his own in the Shōnai area, a development which the Shimazu could not tolerate. In 1602, Shimazu Iehisa dramatically quelled the Shōnai Rebellion, a revolt led by Tadamune's son Tadazane, by having Tadazane murdered during a hunting expedition.

However, Shimazu Iehisa faced discontent among several senior Shimazu retainers, whose resentment found expression in opposing the overall plan for an expedition against Okinawa, as well as the fine details of its execution. Their concerns over what could be a foolhardy venture served to highlight the fact that the seemingly united Shimazu family was in reality split into three separate factions loyal to the current *daimyo* and his predecessors. The three groupings were called the Kagoshima-kata, the Kokubu-kata and the Kajiki-kata; they were associated with the castles of Tsurumaru (Kagoshima) commanded personally by Shimazu Iehisa; Shinshiro (Kokubu) under Shimazu Yoshihisa, and Kajiki under Shimazu Yoshihiro. Iehisa's decision not to lead the army in person may well have taken into account the danger of leaving his fief without its leader, but some of the fiercest opposition to the plans concerned the man that Iehisa had chosen to act in his stead. The leader selected for the invasion

The veteran general of Satsuma, Niiro Musashi-no-kami, is shown here in the frontispiece to *Ehon Ryūkyū Gunki*. In the *gunkimono* accounts of the Okinawa operation he is credited with leading the raid. He actually never left Kagoshima, but the real leader, Kabayama Hisataka, would have looked very similar to this dramatic depiction.

was Kabayama Gonza'emonnojō Hisataka, a man whose family would be associated with Ryūkyū for many years to come. His descendant, Kabayama Sukenori, became the first Japanese governor of Formosa (Taiwan) in 1895, but almost nothing is known of the earlier Kabayama. In accounts of the raid he is an almost anonymous figure, even more shadowy than his second-in-command Hirata Tarōza'emonnojō Masamune. The retainer band opposed Hisataka's appointment over Masamune, stressing the fact that Kabayama Hisataka was the younger of the two men, but the dispute was eventually resolved at a meeting of the senior retainers on 2m 6d of the 14th Year of Keichō (11 March 1609). Hisataka was about to yield his position on the raised dais, the seat of honour, to Masamune when the octogenarian Niiro Musashi-no-kami Tadamoto, the most respected among the Shimazu elders, took Hisataka by the hand and made him take his rightful place. From that moment on, all opposition to Hisataka's appointment ceased.

During the Okinawa raid, Kabayama Hisataka took the place of the *daimyo* himself in his accepted military role as the *sōtaishō*. The *hatamoto* guard was directly accountable to him, while command of the troops of the line, comprising samurai and *ashigaru* footsoldiers, was delegated to *taishō* or *bugashira*. The troops fought in units called *kumi* (-gumi when used as a suffix), and by 1609 even the elite mounted samurai, expressed as a number of *ki*, now served in organised groups rather than fighting in individual combat. The *ashigaru* were arranged in squads, organised according to weapon type, and sub-units of all the divisions fell under the command of officers called either *kumigashira* or *monogashira*.

The other type of role that could be assigned to a senior vassal or family member was that of a *bugyō* who, instead of leading the fighting units, carried out various service support functions, acting as the commander's general staff. Their number would include men in charge of equipment, provisions and supervision of communications. An important role during the Okinawa operation would have been performed by the *fune bugyō*, who took charge of all matters relating to transport on water. Holding a position equivalent in prestige were the *ikusa metsuke*. As well as identifying acts of bravery and cowardice, they would investigate and assess whether

Tanegashima Daisen, the commander of the left vanguard of the Satsuma army, contemplates the fortress on Okinawa that he is about to capture. As befits the lord of the island on which European firearms first arrived, he is shown holding a smoking pistol in his right hand. This is from an 1868 compilation version of *Ehon Ryūkyū Gunki* called *Ehon Ryūkyū Gunki Mokuroku*, illustrated by Ogata Gekkō (1859–1920).

any ambiguous claims of glorious achievement were true or false. While this particular samurai obsession with individual prowess kept them very busy, other tasks included the counting of heads and the identification of both victim and victor.

Much less is known about the commanders and sub-commanders in the Ryūkyūan defence forces. King Shō Nei of Ryūkyū had inherited the military system set up by his illustrious predecessor King Shō Shin (1465–1526), who had ruled from 1477. Throughout his long reign, Shō Shin had tried very successfully to control the power of the *aji*, who were the hereditary warlords of Ryūkyū. At the same time he managed to develop and strengthen an efficient centralised military system, a process that required a delicate balancing act. To achieve the first, Shō Shin required all the *aji* to reside in Shuri, where he bestowed upon them titles and prestige. A similar system would later be used by the *shoguns* of Tokugawa to control the *daimyo*. The *aji*'s former military roles were then taken by government appointees who were directly accountable to the king, while their weapons were collected and stored centrally in Shuri. At the heart of the Ryūkyūan military organisation under Shō Shin were the *hiki*, forces that could be rapidly deployed when danger threatened and who at other times carried out guard and police functions. An official was also appointed to oversee the development of artillery, a matter in which the Ryūkyūan kings had always taken an interest.

King Shō Nei took no part in the fighting during the raid on his country. The closest member of the royal family involved in action was the king's younger brother, who, at the northern fortress of Nakijin, was subjected to the Shimazu's first assault on Okinawa. At the time of the 1609 raid, the names that often appeared in the context of military leadership were those of the members of the king's *sanshikan* (Council of Three) – his closest advisers and occasional *de facto* rulers of the kingdom. In 1609 these were Jana Teidō, Urasoe Chōshi and Nago Ryōhō. Jana Teidō was an accomplished general and a successful administrator, who had spent time in his youth in China. His son-in-law led the resistance on Tokunoshima.

Army Organisation and Troop Numbers

The army of the Shimazu *daimyo* consisted of two categories of soldier, the samurai and the *ashigaru*. The samurai were the knights of old Japan. Traditionally they had been the only warriors to own and ride horses and, centuries earlier, their primary role had been to act as mounted archers. This skill was much less evident on the battlefield by 1609. The usual samurai weapon at the time of the raid was the *yari*, which differed from a European knight's lance in that it was lighter and shorter, and was not carried in a crouched position.

The *ashigaru* were the footsoldiers of a Japanese army. Well-trained and disciplined, they had evolved over the past century from being casually recruited peasant warriors to becoming the lower ranks of the samurai class, a position that was to be formalised under the Tokugawa. Most *ashigaru* were organised in homogeneous groups according to the type of weapon carried: spear, arquebus or bow. The bravest *ashigaru* acted as standard bearers or served as the *daimyo*'s closest attendants, and it would only be in cases of dire emergency that trained *ashigaru* would be used for menial tasks like general baggage carrying, for which purpose numerous labourers were employed. The *ashigaru* were trained to fight in formation. The spearmen usually provided a defence for the missile troops, but could also act in an offensive capacity with their long spears.

While attendants were supplied to a samurai according to his rank, an exclusive body of samurai and *ashigaru* would have attended the general himself, providing

OVERLEAF
These Shimazu samurai and footsoldiers are dressed in Japanese armour of the highest quality attained during its development, with bulletproof breastplates and sturdy helmets. General Kabayama Hisataka **(1)** wears fine armour of a traditional, even old-fashioned style. His *hatamoto* guards **(2)** are distinguished by wearing a golden fan as their *sashimono* (insignia). Even the *ashigaru* **(3)** are well protected.

personal services on a larger scale. These would include a *zori tori*, who, among other duties equivalent to an officer's batman, carried footwear; grooms to lead the general's horse; and other *ashigaru* to carry his provisions, helmet and weapons. Many illustrations show *ashigaru* in the *hatamoto* carrying flags, armour boxes, quivers or an assortment of spears with very elaborate ornamental scabbards.

Written sources are contradictory with regard to the numbers of soldiers used by both sides in the Okinawa operation. Accounts cite a complement of between 1,000 and 3,000 Ryūkyūans mounting a defence against Satsuma. Jana Teidō, for example, commanded 3,000 men in the defence of Naha Harbour. The numbers given for the defence of Amami-Oshima are also 3,000 with 100 for Tokunoshima, but these are the only figures that exist.

The Satsuma accounts give far more detail for the numbers of the aggressors. The overall strength of the expeditionary force depended, as was usual with any *daimyo*'s army, on the assessed wealth of the domain and how much of it should be devoted to a military operation. The unit of measurement was the *koku*, an amount of rice commonly regarded as that needed to feed one man for one year. In the case of the Shimazu, the working total was 402,180.5 *koku*, of which 75,000 *koku* was earmarked for the invasion. Iehisa's retainers were required to supply two men for every 100 *koku* of their recorded wealth, making a total of 1,500 men. The remaining 320,700 *koku* was raised from the inhabitants of the province, who were required to supply in total 107 *kanme* 900 *monme* (404.62kg) of silver together with supplies in the form of army rice to feed 1,500 men.

Even though the retainer band was required to furnish 1,500 men, the number who went to Okinawa is commonly believed to be 3,000 men, conveyed on about 100 ships. Confirmation of this is given in *Kyan Nikki* which records that there were 100 samurai within a total force of 3,000 men conveyed on more than 70 ships. Kyan was well informed, and is likely to have obtained this figure from the Satsuma officials with whom he was to be closely associated after the invasion. In contrast the Satsuma eyewitness, Ichiki Magobe'e Iemoto, makes no mention of the size of the army, saying only that it was conveyed on more than 80 ships. It is possible, however, that Kyan may have been estimating the size of the army, and his figure of 100 samurai may have simply been an observation of mounted troops. Furthermore, it is not clear whether the the figure of 3,000 refers to the total headcount of soldiers, ships' crews and labourers who sailed from Satsuma, or to the actual tally of fighting men. Similarly, there is no indication whether the smaller number of 1,500 relates only to samurai or whether it also includes their personal followers.

A detailed list of the numbers of men supplied by named retainers appears in *Ryūkyū Toshū*, showing that almost all the members of the retainer band exceeded their actual obligations. So, for example, the general of the invasion, Kabayama Hisataka, had to supply 54 men according to the ordnance, but actually supplied 60. A certain Murao Genza'emon Nyudō is listed as being required to supply 'two men, but besides this two men, making four men'. Similar notes appear next to the names of 66 other leaders who supplied 713 men in total. A separate Shimazu document provides a corresponding list of names that gives the figure of more than 100 samurai in an army of

9 APRIL 1609

Fleet reaches Kuchinoerabujima

The Heiromon, one of the main gates of the *gusuku* of Nakijin, the first castle to be attacked by the Shimazu on mainland Okinawa. There gunports on either side of the entrance, evidence of successive Ryūkyūan kings' expertise with early firearms. Where they did not keep pace with the times was in the European-style deployment of massed ranks of arquebuses.

3,000 men conveyed on 100 ships. Reference to 3,000 men on 100 ships also appears in a third document.

A different army listing appears in another Shimazu document where Kabayama's general staff are named according to which of the three 'factions', the Kagoshima-kata, the Kokubu-kata or the Kajiki-kata, they belonged. The Kagoshima-kata provided the three *bugyō* who went with the army – two *heigu bugyō* in charge of the army and strategy, one *fune bugyō* for sea transport and three *bugashira*. From the Kokubu-kata came nine *bugashira*, and a further four were supplied by the Kajiki-kata. There was also an army priest, together with over 100 unspecified samurai and 30 bearers of weapons. To these were added ships' carpenters.

The deployment of *ashigaru* weapon groups made use of fighting men in a reserve capacity, so it would not have been difficult to amass a total of 3,000 fighting men. However, as 100 ships would need a large number of crewmen, it is highly improbable the latter were included in the documented total of 3,000. Porters, labourers and boatmen would have also added to the number. In Korea in 1592, about 65% of a typical *daimyo*'s manpower quota could have been made up from non-combatant staff. In one detailed example, Gotō Sumiharu sent 220 fighting men to Korea with 485 men in supporting functions. A similar percentage is found on analysing the contingent that was supposed to accompany Shimazu Yoshihiro to Korea in 1592, when the army of Satsuma should have consisted of 600 samurai and 3,600 *ashigaru* out of a grand total of 15,000 men. The number actually supplied by Satsuma was 10,000, not 15,000, indicating that after being defeated by Hideyoshi in 1587, the Shimazu simply could not meet the obligation. Yet even 10,000 men for a seaborne expedition in 1592 was a much larger number than the 3,000 assembled by the Satsuma in 1609. This may have meant they were in even more desperate financial circumstances after their defeat at Sekigahara. Alternatively, as they were able to field another large army of 10,000 for the siege of Osaka in 1614, it is more likely this figure was all they felt was necessary to conquer Ryūkyū in a short and decisive operation.

As a final note on troop numbers and organisation, useful information may be gleaned from the *gunkimono*. *Shimazu Ryūkyū Gunseiki* appears remarkably precise and very valuable. It lists every general's name and gives a breakdown of his followers according to weapon groups. When combined with *Ehon Ryūkyū Gunki*, which is effectively an illustrated version of the *gunkimono*, one is given a complete and detailed account of each unit of the invading army, including each general's individual heraldry and even the heraldic device on the sails of his ship. Unfortunately it is not a useful historical source, because the names of the generals do not correspond to the names in the reliable household accounts, nor do the figures of the troops they are said to command add up. Tanegashima Daisen, who is named as commanding the left wing of the vanguard, is shown as having troops numbering 4,106, but the subtotal written at the end of his section is almost four times greater at 20,370. The grand total for the Shimazu army using such subtotals works out at an astounding 103,770 men, which may be compared with the 10,000 they sent to Korea as part of a total Japanese army of 138,000, drawn from all the *daimyo* that took part.

If the numbers are unreliable, the breakdown of the army by weaponry and organisation may contain more useful information. The Shimazu family documents, although precise about the names of the *bugyō* and *bugashira* in separate, matching accounts, reveal a complete lack of understanding as to how the army was actually arranged. *Shimazu Ryūkyū Gunseiki*, however, describes the army being split into different *sonae* of vanguard (left and right), 2nd (left and right), 3rd, 4th, 5th, 6th and rearguard. This matches very similar arrangements noted for other armies of the period, so is likely to be based on fact in all but the total numbers of troops. As for the internal organisation of the *sonae*, this is again addressed in *Shimazu Ryūkyū Gunseiki*, where Tanegashima Daisen is said to command three *ashigaru* units of equal numbers of spears, bows and guns, all led by *monogashira*. There is also reference to a squad armed with axes and, for signalling purposes, with war drums and bells. Samurai, both mounted and on foot, are described, as well as a designated rearguard for the division. Equipment in other *sonae* includes *kumade* and conch shell trumpets. The other *sonae* are similarly arranged, except that the 6th *sonae*, the main body under Niiro Musashi-no-kami, contains the sole mention of flag carriers. All the numbers cited are very large, and, as already noted, are not internally consistent. The grand total of the army is swollen by the inclusion of a huge number of named samurai and their followers in the rearguard, and additionally, no fewer than eight named warriors with the family name of Shimazu, all with huge retinues (one having 10,000 samurai to himself). There are also five *metsuke*, in accordance with what one might expect, and an interesting breakdown of the non-combatant support function, including the men in charge of storing rice, followed by those who transport it by packhorse, cart or on their own backs.

Based on the available evidence, an estimate of the likely size and composition of the Shimazu army is as follows:

General Staff	
General	
Second-in-Command	
Bugyō	3
Bugashira	16
Attendants	100
Mounted Samurai	100
Attendants	200
Foot Samurai	700
Ashigaru	
Arquebus	800
Spear	800
Bow	300
Others	200
Total fighting troops	3,000
Labourers	2,000
Sailors	3,000

It is likely that around 3,000 fighting men with 5,000 supporters went to Okinawa. These figures are one-fifteenth of the number cited in *Shimazu Ryūkyū Gunseiki*.

Arms and Armour

The Shimazu samurai and *ashigaru* were well armed and well armoured. The samurai were predominately spearmen with swords as a secondary weapon. The blades of the *yari* spears were very sharp on both edges, with their tangs sunk into stout oak shafts. This made the *yari* into a weapon unsuitable for slashing but ideal for stabbing – the best technique to use from a saddle. A useful variation was a cross-bladed spear that enabled a samurai to pull an opponent from his horse. If a samurai wished to deliver slashing strokes from horseback then a better choice than a *yari* was the *naginata*, a polearm with a long curved blade, or the spectacular *nodachi*, a very long sword with a very strong and very long handle. When having to fight dismounted,

OVERLEAF

This general of the Okinawa army (1) wears a mixture of Chinese and Japanese styles. His troops (2) are more simply dressed in armour of the *haramaki* style, open at the back. Some carry the simple three-barrelled firearms (3) favoured by the Ryūkyūans. Their use of swords differs from the Japanese, as they wield the short *wakizashi* in one hand and carry a small shield in the other. They fight under the 'three commas' flag of the king of Ryūkyū.

the *yari* would be a samurai's primary weapon of choice, as was evidenced on Okinawa. There are no references in the literature to cavalry charges, but horses would have been well used in the rapid movement overland.

The samurai's other main weapon was, of course, the famous *katana*. This classic samurai sword would be forged to perfection, with a razor-sharp edge within a resilient body. Every samurai possessed at least one pair of swords, the *katana* and the shorter *wakizashi*. Both seem to have been carried into battle along with a *tantō* (dagger). The samurai never used shields; instead, the *katana* acted as both sword and shield, its resilience enabling the samurai to deflect a blow aimed at him by knocking the attacking sword to one side with the flat of the blade, and then following up with a stroke of his own.

Samurai wore strong and flexible armour. The traditional style of manufacture had been for the armour plates to be made from individual iron or leather scales laced together. By 1609, the design had been modified to solid-plate body armour, thus giving better protection against gunfire. Lamellar sections, however, continued to be found in both thigh and shoulder guards. Armoured arm sleeves and shin guards protected the limbs. Above the neck would be the most striking part of a samurai's armour – an iron mask to protect the face. A moustache made of horsehair was often added to the mask and the mouthpiece decorated with a sinister grin around white teeth. The helmet was very solid, but senior samurai, and many *daimyo*, would use the design of the helmet crown to give a personal touch to what was otherwise very practical protection, using wood and papier-mâché to build up the surface into fantastic shapes.

The other way in which an individual samurai or *ashigaru* would be recognised in the heat of battle was by wearing a small identifying device on his back, called a *sashimono*. This would often be in the form of a flag in a wooden holder, displaying the *daimyo*'s *mon* on a coloured background so that the unit could easily be recognised. While this would apply to most rank-and-file samurai, senior samurai would be allowed to have their own *mon*, or sometimes their family name, displayed on the flag. Golden fans and plumes of feathers could replace the small flag, but the most spectacular form of *sashimono* was the *horo*. This was a cloak stretched over a bamboo framework that had become a decorative appendage for a *daimyo*'s elite samurai who acted as *tsukai-ban* (courier guards). The *horo* filled with air as he rode across the battlefield, and the bright colours made him visible to friend and foe. There is evidence that excellent communications were maintained between separate units of the Satsuma army on Okinawa, and the *tsukai-ban* would have been crucial in achieving this. The *ashigaru* wore simple suits of iron armour, usually consisting of a body armour from which hung a skirt of protective plates. The breastplate bore the *mon* of the *daimyo*, a device that also appeared on the simple lampshade-shaped helmet known as the *jingasa*. Armour protection for the arms and calves was also often provided.

All accounts of the 1609 operation stress the vital role played by firearms in the Shimazu advance. As befitted the rulers of the province that had witnessed the arrival of the first European-style firearms on Japanese shores in 1543, the

The use of volley firing by squads of *ashigaru* armed with arquebuses was a decisive factor in the victory achieved by the Shimazu over the Ryūkyū Kingdom. Arquebuses are shown here in the hands of a precisely dressed re-enactment group at Oshi castle in 2006.

Shimazu army had never been behind the times in gunpowder technology. Like all other Japanese *daimyo*, however, their use of firearms was largely confined to the hand-held arquebus rather than cannon. The Shimazu, in fact, seem to have suffered the consequences of cannon more than most, having twice come under fire from European-made big guns owned by the Otomo at the battles of Mimigawa in 1578 and Usuki in 1586. Yet in spite of their previous experiences, the Shimazu do not appear to have taken the heavy weaponry of a siege train with them to Okinawa. Instead, just as in the case of Korea in 1592, hundreds of bullets were to pour from the muzzles of the guns held by the well-disciplined *ashigaru* in the Shimazu army. The arquebus was fired when a smouldering match, fastened into a serpentine, was dropped onto the touch-hole. To prevent premature discharges, the touch-hole was closed until the point of firing by a tight-fitting brass cover. One disadvantage of the arquebus was its slow loading time compared to the bow, making it necessary for archers to provide cover while reloading took place. The experience of the battle of Nagashino in 1575 had confirmed volley firing as the most effective way of using the arquebus, but it also illustrated the iron-hard discipline needed to make it work.

The inclusion of bows in the Shimazu army shows that even at this late stage in samurai warfare, archers were still prized. Some may have been highly trained sharpshooters used as skirmishers or for sniping, but their most important role was to fire volleys of arrows. Even though bows had a shorter range than the arquebus and required a more experienced operator, their rate of fire was more rapid and enemy arrows could be re-used. Archers were supported by carriers who were at hand with large quiver boxes, each containing 100 arrows. The preferred range for firing was from 30 to 80m, and the bow had a maximum effective range of 380m.

The earliest *ashigaru* spears had been the same length as samurai ones, and were wielded just as freely in the conflicts of the Onin War. From about 1530 onwards, the shaft of the *ashigaru* weapon lengthened noticeably, producing the *nagae-yari* that was more akin to a pike. The *ashigaru* spearmen were trained to fight as a group, formed up in a line of two or three ranks with their spearpoints even, thus showing certain similarities to European pikemen. Other *ashigaru* units included players of drums, bells and conch shell trumpets, wielders of rakes and axes and importantly, bearers of flags. Long banners called *nobori* were used for the identification of units, while the *daimyo*'s *uma jirushi* (battle-standards) would attract some of the fiercest fighting. Visual communications depended largely on the use of flags, while the *uma jirushi* and massed *nobori* played a vital role in orientation on a battlefield.

Ignoring the obvious exaggerations of total numbers, the weaponry described in *Shimazu Ryūkyū Gunseiki* does not differ significantly from that described in the only other guide on the subject, a brief summary within the Shimazu archives of the weaponry supplied for the army. Curiously, spears are not mentioned:

Arquebuses	734
Bullets	37,200
Bows	117
Quivers	117
Bowstrings	351 (two spare bowstrings per bow)
Kuwa	397
Axes, hatchets, other tools	398

Kuwa were sickle blades mounted on long shafts, which would have been useful for sea fighting should the Ryūkyūan navy have tried to intercept the raid. Axes and hatchets would have been employed for construction projects and siege work, and may have been used by non-combatant labourers. The number of arquebuses implies that the Shimazu put great faith in the power of bullets when delivered in controlled volleys, and may be compared in number to the 1,500 arquebuses used by the larger Shimazu army of 1592 in Korea, an operation that confirmed the devastating effects of mass volleys from firearms. By means of such tactics, the Japanese invaders had taken Korean walled cities without lengthy sieges, a point that must have been in the mind of Kabayama Hisataka when he made preparations to deploy his army against the castles of Okinawa, which also had low walls, low parapets and little opportunity for defensive fire. Controlled volleys would have swept the defenders from their parapets, allowing the samurai to mount scaling ladders and fight their way onto the walls.

A written compilation of *daimyo* heraldry, *O Uma Jirushi*, produced early in the Edo Period, includes reference to Shimazu Iehisa and this gives a very good indication as to how the Shimazu army on Okinawa would have appeared overall. The designs shown are very similar to contemporary illustrations on painted screens of the Shimazu army at the battle of Sekigahara. Because Kabayama Hisataka led the army on Iehisa's behalf, it is reasonable to assume that the force had the same overall appearance as if the *daimyo* himself were present. General Kabayama, in accordance with his rank, would have worn an elaborate suit of armour, although no details of it have survived. The *o uma jirushi* (great battle-standard) of the Shimazu was a three-dimensional bunch of black cock's feathers. The *nobori* banners were diagonally divided in two, with black below and white above, and bore the Shimazu *mon* of a black cross in a ring (said to be derived from the shape of a horse's bit, and with no Christian connotations whatsoever) in the upper section. One particularly large *nobori* acted as the *ko uma jirushi* (lesser battle-standard). This *nobori* had a small flag attached to it that was white with the Shimazu *mon*. One interesting feature of Kabayama Hisataka's *hatamoto* was their use of a *sashimono* that was not a flag. Instead it was a wooden gold-lacquered fan. The samurai in the line infantry and the *ashigaru* would, however, have worn flag *sashimono*, more typically consisting of a flag with a white background on which was inscribed the *mon*, or the same with colours reversed. Tools would have been wielded by non-combatant labourers who, although unlikely to have been wearing armour, may well have been issued with a *jingasa*. The *mon* of the Shimazu is likely to have been stencilled on to their coats.

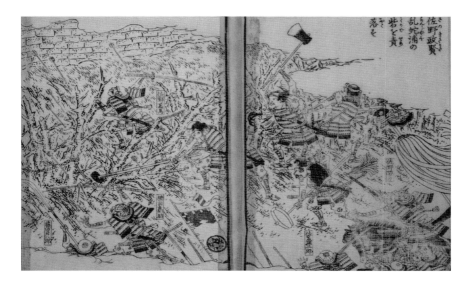

The 5th *sonae* of the Shimazu army, under Sano Masakata, attacks an Okinawan fortress under a hail of arrows, cutting its way through rudimentary defences of tree branches using axes, hammers and mallets.(ERG)

The details of the arms and armour of the defenders of Ryūkyū are very sketchy when compared to the information available for the invaders. From written accounts, one may conclude that although the Ryūkyūan weapons were not as good as those of Satsuma, they were by no means primitive. It is well established that the Ryūkyūans conducted trade between China and Japan involving weapons. However during the 1450s, these armaments were needed at home to defend against *wakō*, so the inhabitants of Fujian province in China were banned from selling weapons to Ryūkyū in private dealings. The Japanese sword was valued as much on Okinawa as it was in China, but it is known that adaptations were made to the weapon by fitting it with a handle that would allow fighting with one hand. As the long *katana* would not have been practical in this regard, it is assumed that new handles were fitted to the shorter *wakizashi*. Small wooden shields were sometimes carried in the left hand. The Ryūkyūan forces were likely, therefore, to have presented a mix of Chinese and Japanese armaments, deploying bows, swords, spears and guns. Halberds, either the broad bladed Chinese version or the very similar Japanese *naginata* with blades more akin to swords, were also used.

The kings of Ryūkyū had also been early converts to firearms. The shipwrecked Koreans of 1450 noted that the Ryūkyūan use of firearms was similar to their own even at that early stage. These would have been the short-barrelled weapons obtained from China, which were made with a short iron tube fixed to a long wooden shaft. The barrel was wider round its touch-hole and had a slightly conical muzzle terminating in an elongated aperture. Pictures of similar European models show the stock of the gun being held tightly under the left arm while the right hand applied the lighted match. This type of gun is known to have been used in Japan as late as 1548 at the battle of Uedahara, but it was never widely adopted in Japanese warfare and

A mounted officer in the Ryūkyūan army, depicted in armour of the Chinese Ming dynasty, is cornered by a group of Satsuma samurai, who stab him with their spears and attempt to drag him from his horse using *kumade*. (ERG)

was immediately scrapped when the much more sophisticated model based on the European arquebus came into general use. A popular version used on Ryūkyū had three barrels. It is highly probable the Ryūkyūans were aware of the existence of the European-style arquebus, even though Kyan's diary refers to the battle at Tairabashi with the words: 'The enemy attacked the bridge in a hail of bullets. We did not know about guns like these.' Such a remark probably indicates his unfamiliarity with volley-firing techniques. It is known that the Ryūkyūans possessed cannon of a type known as *ishibiya*, a name later given to artillery that fired a shot of one *kanme* (3.75kg) or more. This is consistent with shot of between 7 and 9cm in diameter that has been excavated from the site of Shuri Castle. Cannon were also mounted in the defences of Naha Port.

No examples of Ryūkyūan armour have survived, but in the illustrations prepared for *Ehon Ryūkyū Gunki* in about 1802, the artist depicted the generals of Okinawa wearing Chinese-style armour, resembling officers of the Great Ming. It may have been artistic convention to represent the soldiers of a kingdom regarded by most Japanese as wonderfully exotic in this way, but the illustrations could well reflect an element of truth. Even though this is a work of historical fiction based on the exaggerated *gunkimono* accounts of the raid, representations of samurai armour and equipment are meticulous in their detail. Generals on Okinawa are also shown wearing a mixture of Chinese and Japanese armour, often with a Japanese-style *jinbaori* (surcoat) and the use of a helmet not unlike the *jingasa* of the Japanese *ashigaru*. Other Ryūkyūan warriors wore Japanese-style *haramaki* armour that was open at the back. Lower-class warriors on Okinawa were more simply dressed and wore no defensive armour. Instead they appear to have worn the ordinary attire common in Ryūkyū, consisting of a *kimono*-like robe tied at the waist, and a headcloth. Ryūkyūan soldiers marched under the 'three commas' banner of their kings and other triangular embroidered flags in the Chinese style. Long trumpets and war drums provided their musical accompaniment.

Both the Ryūkyūans and the Shimazu were great sailors, with active sea communications between the numerous islands they each controlled and contested. The ships that conveyed the Satsuma army to Okinawa would have been of two types, the *ataka bune* and the *sengoku bune*. The *ataka bune* were the warships of any *daimyo*'s navy and had been employed as troop transports and (much less successfully) as warships during the invasion of Korea. No *ataka bune* has survived, but combined with a few illustrations on painted screens, it is possible to reconstruct their appearance with great accuracy. A typical *ataka bune* looked like a floating wooden box. The whole of the side surface was one blank wall of thick wooden planks which protected the oarsmen and the samurai, and was pierced with small loopholes for guns and bows. The open upper deck was shielded by a low bulwark that was, in fact, an extension of the side walls. In some versions a cabin, again very solidly built, sat on the deck. In addition to the oar propulsion, there was a mast from which a large sail was hung bearing the *daimyo*'s *mon* in a bold stencilled or painted design. In a manner typical of most Japanese ships of the time, the mast was pivoted centrally and very delicately balanced so that, using rollers on top of the supports, it could be folded down when the ship went into action. The normal complement of an *ataka bune* was 80 oarsmen and 60 fighting men, with three cannon and 30 arquebuses. The sleeker *sengoku bune* (1,000-*koku* ship) was the workaday transport of the Edo Period, and these were pressed into service for the raid. Like the *ataka bune*, the ships would have been ornamented with the Shimazu *mon* stencilled onto the middle of their sails.

11 APRIL 1609

Armed landing on Amami-Oshima

20 APRIL 1609

Amami-Oshima pacified

THE PLAN

The Shimazu Strategy

The overall Shimazu strategy, which was followed almost to the letter, was to secure the Amami Islands and then establish a beachhead on Okinawa. From there, two armies would move rapidly southwards, one by sea to secure Naha Port, the other by land to take Shuri Castle when Naha had fallen. To reach Okinawa, the Shimazu had to assemble their forces from a wide area across Satsuma, Hyūga and Osumi and then embark them at a suitable harbour. The voyage would not need to be made entirely across open seas, because the friendly Tokara Islands, together with Yakishima, Tanegashima and Kuchierabujima, could provide possible protection and safe harbour in the event of bad weather at the start of the operation.

The scheme was a major military undertaking with great potential risk, and Shimazu Iehisa impressed upon Hisataka that he was to avoid a prolonged campaign. Iehisa wished at all costs to avoid a lengthy siege of Shuri Castle, which was both the royal palace and the strongest fortress on Okinawa, and was linked to the fortified harbour of Naha by a military road. If a long siege seemed likely then Hisataka was to burn the town of Shuri, withdraw from Okinawa and occupy the surrounding islands including Amami-Oshima. There were two reasons for the need to move quickly. The first took into account the seasonal winds, that could prove difficult and dangerous for ships crossing to Okinawa. The second related to the presence of men within the Shimazu retainer band who were opposed to the idea of an invasion and whose political position would be strengthened by a long and expensive campaign.

Defensive Preparations

The failure of the negotiations in 1608 had alerted the Ryūkyūans to expect threatening moves by the Shimazu. It may be they thought the Satsuma advance would be limited to the Amami Islands, because references describe reinforcements being made ready to sail to Amami-Oshima and Tokunoshima. When news was received of the rapid fall of the islands, these plans were abandoned.

The main island of Okinawa had long been well defended. Since the 14th century, a number of formidable stone castles, known in the Ryūkyūan dialect as *gusuku*, dotted the landscape. Most were built in positions overlooking the sea and covering the approach to harbours. The topography of Okinawa is such that no one place is far from the sea and by 1609, a patchwork of *gusuku* spread from Nakijin in the north down to Tamagusuku on the southern coast. In their design the *gusuku* were quite unlike traditional Japanese castles. In many respects their walls resembled those of Korean and Chinese castles, even if they did not always follow hill contours like the Great Wall of China to make a *sanseong* in the Korean style. Instead they enclosed successive baileys on a hillside, within which administrative buildings were built from wood. At the time of the rivalry between the 'Three Kingdoms' of Hokuzan, Chūzan and Nanzan, the *gusuku* had been the focus of much military activity.

While the *gusuku* were expected to hinder any advance by land, the harbour defences of Naha Port were designed to prevent assaults from the sea, and respond to the threat posed by the *wakō*. These savage pirates, whose name implied that they came specifically from the 'Country of Wa', in other words Japan, were international freebooters who treated all countries with contempt, including Ryūkyū. The native inhabitants of Okinawa and the other smaller islands did not welcome them, particularly when the pirates disguised themselves as legitimate traders, but as the Ryūkyū Islands were so extensive, it was not difficult for the *wakō* to find safe anchorages without being molested. At least one *gusuku*, the castle of Gushikawa on the island of Kumejima, has been identified from archaeological finds as a pirate base. The more remote islands of the Yaeyama group also provided staging posts and moorings for *wakō*. Kabira Bay on Ishigaki Island was one such safe anchorage, as was the island of Iriomote, where pirates took refuge along the rivers that led into its jungle-covered interior.

On two occasions, once in 1553 and again in 1556, the defenders of Naha Port had driven off *wakō* raids. These successes were due largely to the well-planned harbour defences that two kings had commissioned. In 1522, King Shō Shin had built a military road between Naha and Shuri so that troops could be moved rapidly between the two key positions of the main harbour and the palace. A few years later, in 1546, King Shō Sei had ordered the building of a small castle on each side of the harbour entrance. The two fortresses were called Yarazamori and Mie, and were linked by an iron chain that could be raised in the case of an attack. Yarazamori, the larger of the two, was a rectangular structure of stone walls in the characteristic style of the Okinawan *gusuku*, and had been built with sixteen regularly spaced loopholes for cannon. The southern approach to Naha and Shuri was defended by a castle called Tomigusuku (today the site of Tomigusuku City). As events were to prove, when the impressive-looking *gusuku*, failed to stop the overland advance, the concentration of defensive efforts around the harbour turned out to be Okinawa's undoing.

A mounted single combat between a Satsuma samurai armed with a impossibly large iron club and a senior Ryūkyūan warrior, depicted here in Chinese armour and armed with a straight-bladed sword. (ERG)

THE RAID

The Battle for the Amami Islands

The Shimazu army departed from Satsuma province for Okinawa on 3m 4d (8 April 1609). Of the three eyewitness accounts, Ichiki Magobe'e Iemoto provides the first description of the operation, beginning with the time he left his home in Takayama on the last day of the second lunar month (4 April). He describes his arrival on 3m 1d (5 April) at the point of embarkation, which was Yamakawa, a small harbour at the end of the peninsula to the south of Kagoshima. Ichiki's contingent must have been among the last to arrive, because the army had been assembling since 2m 6d (11 March). His narrative continues until his return to Yamakawa on 4m 28d of the same year (31 May), his part in the entire Ryūkyū conquest from leaving home to returning having been completed in less than two months.

The progress of the army from Satsuma to Okinawa was greatly helped by the fact that the first half of their voyage took place through friendly waters. The Satsuma expeditionary force set sail from Yamakawa on 3m 4d (8 April) and arrived the following day at the island of Kuchinoerabujima, where they stayed overnight. From there, they set out two days later on the voyage to Amami-Oshima and their first taste of military action, sailing past the friendly Tokara Islands. The narrative from the Satsuma perspective, entitled *Ryūkyū Gunki*, was written by a sea-captain from this region. Reports written about the early part of the operation give the impression that the contingent from the Tokara Islands did not join the fleet en route but had assembled with everyone else at Yamakawa some time previously.

The first shots of the campaign were fired against Ryūkyūan defenders when landfall was made at the northern tip of the island of Oshima, the largest of the Amami group, on 3m 7d (11 April). This took place at Fukue ga Ura on Kasari Bay. The priest Kyan, who was on Okinawa when Amami-Oshima was attacked, notes only that on Amami-Oshima the defending army had grown weak. While he makes no other comment about the operation to secure the Amami Islands, Ichiki reports that on the following day, the Shimazu forces went out on patrol and easily overcame the islanders, who fought under a certain 'Zōhon of Kasari', the Okinawan king's representative on Oshima. The invaders then made their way by ship along the coast to Yamatohama, where they arrived on 3m 12d (16 April), and four days later had advanced as far as Nishi Yoshimi, thus securing the whole island. Amami-Oshima, for the first time in two centuries, passed back into Shimazu control.

The impression given by Ichiki is that the Shimazu army met with little serious resistance, but simply took their time to secure control over Amami-Oshima in a nine-day operation. The regaining of the Amami Islands was, of course, the Shimazu's fallback position if a long siege of Shuri Castle made a withdrawal necessary. The anonymous sea-captain, however, paints a very different picture. His *Ryūkyū Gunki* indicates that the invaders met with considerable problems both from the weather and

24 APRIL 1609

Armed landing on Tokunoshima

26 APRIL 1609

Tokunoshima operation concluded

The island of Tokunoshima, one of the Amami Islands, showing the approximate location of the Shimazu landing during the operation of 1609. The invaders met with fierce resistance on Tokunoshima, and there were many casualties among the defenders.

from the islanders. Adverse winds blew 70 out of the 75 ships off course, and the fleet only made it to Oshima after the five ships containing Kabayama Hisataka and the sea-captain himself had landed in dangerous isolation from the rest of the army. Second-in-command Hirata Masamune, offered to send troops to help them, but his assistance was declined. The fleet faced stiff resistance from the islanders, 3,000 of whom mounted a defence from within a wooden stockade, which the Shimazu eventually overcame by employing concentrated arquebus fire.

Further opposition was encountered when the Shimazu army re-embarked for the voyage along the island chain and landed on Tokunoshima. They arrived at Shutoku on 3m 20d (24 April) and advanced to nearby Kametsu. On 3m 22d (26 April), they went into the mountains on a manhunt to seek out and kill the defenders who had regrouped there. Here the Shimazu encountered Ryūkyūans under the command of the son-in-law of Jana Teidō. Between 200 and 300 Ryūkyūan soldiers died in the fierce battle for Tokunoshima. *Ryūkyū Gunki* adds more detail relating how the islanders, led and inspired in their resistance by two brothers, wielded long spears, sharpened bamboo poles, kitchen knives and woodmen's hatchets against the invaders in an unexpected attack that took the lives of 'six or seven men from the Shōnai company'. The Satsuma force rallied and again brought in firearms to achieve control. The elder of the two brothers was shot in the breast while the younger brother continued the fight on the beach and then retreated before he could be captured. Some looting appears to have taken place inside the islanders' houses, where the Satsuma samurai met further resistance from peasants wielding hatchets. On 3m 23d (27 April), the Shimazu tried to intercept a number of Ryūkyūan boats that were seen heading in the direction of Amami-Oshima, but were unable to catch them.

The Okinawa raid: first phase from Satsuma to northern Okinawa.

ACTIONS

1 After gathering forces the Shimazu fleet leaves Yamakawa on 8 April and arrives on friendly Kuchinoerabujima the following day.

2 The first shots of the campaign are fired on Amami-Oshima on 11 April. The army proceeds along the coast and finally pacifies Amami-Oshima on 20 April.

3 Fierce resistance is encountered on Tokunoshima on 24 April.

4 The island of Okinoerabujima surrenders when the rising tide allowed the Satsuma force to land on 28 April.

5 The Shimazu enter the waters off Unten harbour and land on Kourijima and a small island off Okinawa on 29 April.

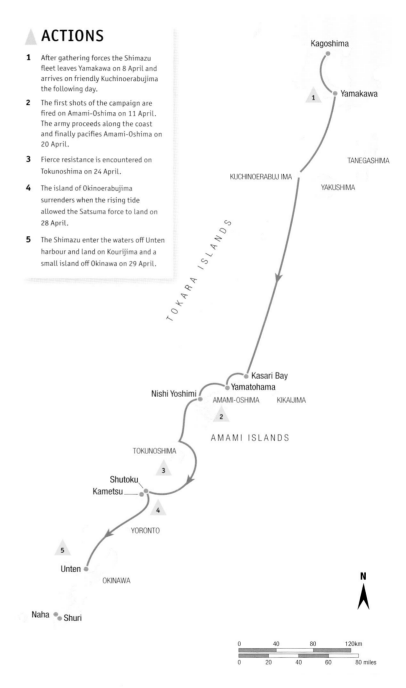

The view from the walls of Nakijin, looking towards the sea. The low walls and parapets of a typical Okinawan *gusuku* are shown clearly here. Nakijin lay in a commanding position on the Motobu peninsula overlooking the strategic harbour of Unten. It was neutralized during the first armed operation after the landing on Okinawa.

The following day, the invaders proceeded to Okinoerabujima, where fierce waves and rocky shallows suggested they would not be able to land. As it happened, a rising tide carried them over these obstacles, and the 'Prince of Okinoerabujima' as the author of *Ryūkyū Gunki* calls him, meekly sent a priest as an envoy with an offer of surrender. This was accepted by General Kabayama with contempt. With Okinoerabujima pacified, the Satsuma invasion force could pause and regroup ready for the main assault. This process took little time. Only one of the Amami Islands now lay between the fleet and Okinawa. This was Yorontō, which Kabayama decided to bypass, and so the Shimazu reached Okinawa on 3m 25d (29 April).

The Battle for Northern Okinawa

The island of Okinawa, as befits its comparison to a rope in the sea, is long and narrow. As the crow flies the distance from its north-eastern tip to its south-western extremity is about 115km (71 miles), but at its narrowest point the neck of land is only about 3km (less than two miles) wide. It was the shape of the island that helped determine the ancient division into the rival principalities of north, central and south. Nowadays the northern part of the island remains the least developed. The central area contains most of Okinawa's celebrated beach resorts and an extensive military presence in the shape of US bases. Naha, which is now the prefectural capital of Okinawa, and the ancient palace of Shuri lie towards the south. The Shimazu plans took careful account of the topography of their target. Landfall was to be made in the north, with the establishment of a base. Two raiding forces would then converge on the king's capital – one overland, the other by sea to secure the port of Naha.

The place selected by the Shimazu for landfall on Okinawa had to be carefully selected because the extreme northerly end of the island provides little opportunity for anchorage. Safe mooring could be found at the large harbour of Unten, which lies in a sheltered position on the north-eastern side of the Motobu peninsula. Protected from the rough seas by the two islands of Kourijima and Yagajishima, it would have been an ideal place for an invasion fleet to make preparations for a further advance. However, sprawled on the hills overlooking Unten and the northern coastline of the peninsula stood the important *gusuku* of Nakijin, while over towards the southern side of the Motobu peninsula was a smaller castle called Nago. As a result, the Shimazu did not enter Unten Harbour directly, but landed on the offshore island of Kourijima, which provided sufficient sheltered anchorage for the fleet between Kourijima and Yagajishima, in a narrow area of sea nowadays crossed by a long road-bridge. No attempt was made by the Ryūkyūans to stop the fleet entering. The islanders clearly did not have the capacity to mount such an attack at that stage, and an urgent message was sent to Shuri requesting reinforcements. These were provided in the form of 1,000 men under the command of Nago Ryōhō.

In its heyday, Nakijin Castle was the largest of the Okinawan *gusuku*. It was built on a natural defensive site, with a sharp cliff dropping to the Shikema River on its eastern side, forest to the south and the sea to the north and north-west. Its construction began at the end of the 13th century, and its graceful curved limestone walls enclosing a series of baileys were typical of the *gusuku* style. Low parapets along the tops of the walls, however, provided the only protection for soldiers stationed along them. There were neither merlons nor loopholes, making them even more vulnerable to attack than the walls around Korean cities that had fallen so rapidly in 1592. The only superstructure along the walls existed above the gateways, which were the castle's strongest points of defence. Two important gates lay on the northern and southern sides respectively. The southern gate (*mon*) was called the Shijimamon, while the northern one was known as the Heiromon and acts as the entrance for visitors to Nakijin today. Over the years, the stonework has been carefully restored, showing the gunports on either side of the entrance and thus confirming the early use of firearms by the Ryūkyūan kings. Initially, guns would have been of the short-barrelled Chinese type but heavier weapons would have been mounted in the gunports by the time of the raid. In 1609, additional wooden structures would have consisted of a lookout tower above the gateway, probably with a thatched roof, and very heavy gates within the stone portals.

During the time of the 'Three Kingdoms', Nakijin had been the capital of Hokuzan, the northernmost of the three rival principalities and a lively centre for trade with China. Nakijin fell to Shō Hashi in 1416, who sent his younger brother to take command of the northern part of the newly united kingdom in 1422. The brother was given the title of

The graceful sweep of the walls of the *gusuku* of Nakijin. Here the walls follow the contour of the hill. The walls are made of limestone.

ASSAULT ON THE NAKIJIN FORTRESS
29 APRIL – 2 MAY 1609

The *gusuku* of Nakijin was the first place on the main island of Okinawa to be attacked by the Shimazu army. Here we are looking from the north-west towards land. In the distance lie the islands of Yagajishima and Kourijima that provided shelter for the Shimazu fleet. In close-up we see the Shimazu samurai attacking the Heiromon Gate of Nakijin castle.

NAKIJIN FORTRESS, DEFENCES AND SHIMAZU ADVANCE 1-11

1 Ushimi riding field

2 Heiromon Gate

3 Nakijin *gusuku*

4 Shijimojo gate

5 Yagajishima island

6 Shimazu fleet

7 Kourijima island

8 The *Hatamoto* guards, highly visible to both friend and foe thanks to their gold fan insignia.

9 The *ashigaru* are armed with bows and arrows as well as spears.

10 A Ryūkyū defender fires a three-barrelled firearm through a slit in the wall.

11 The defenders use any weapon possible to defend the Nakijin fortress, including archery, the short *wakizashi* sword and even rocks.

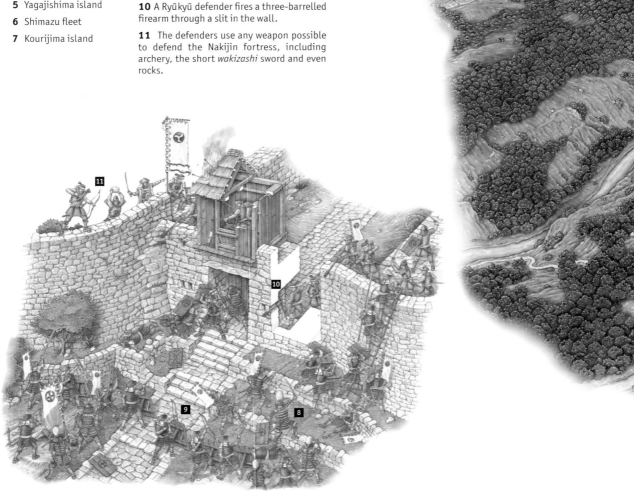

A samurai identified as Hikita Jūza'emon smashes open the gate of 'Yōkeidan castle', which is probably Nakijin, the first fortress on Okinawa to be attacked by the Shimazu. (Original illustration in *Ehon Ryūkyū Gunki Mokuroku* – ERGM)

Hokuzan Kanshi ('Warden of the North'), an important position that was to stay within the royal household, so that in 1609, Nakijin was being defended by Shō Nei's son Shō Kokushi. On hearing of the defeat on Amami-Oshima, Shō Kokushi strengthened the defences of Nakijin and was preparing to send a force to supplement the garrison on Tokunoshima, when the news reached him that they had already fallen to the Shimazu.

The events of the next couple of days are somewhat confusing. The Shimazu had landed on Kourijima on 3m 25d (29 April) and although Nakijin should have proved a real problem for their advance, the island somehow fell to the invaders. Unfortunately, only brief accounts survive of what happened. Ichiki Magobe'e Iemoto cannot have been actively involved in the attack because he says nothing about what occurred on 3m 26d (30 April). He simply records that on 3m 27d (1 May) Hirata Masamune and Ijuin Hisamoto set out from Kourijima to reconnoitre the site of Nakijin only to find it abandoned, and that: 'At the Hour of the Snake they came back having set fire to places around Unten Harbour and raiding the fields that were meticulously maintained.' This implies that the Ryūkyūan army in Nakijin had seen the arrival of the Shimazu and fled in terror, abandoning their posts and leaving Unten Harbour open for the invaders. However, from Okinawan sources there are two statements that suggest fierce resistance took place. The first relates how Nago Ryō hō, who had marched north in support with 1,000 men, met the Shimazu in battle and lost half his army; the second, that on 3m 28d (2 May) Shō Kokushi, the *Hokuzan Kanshi*, died. The cause of death is not given, but was probably due to wounds received during the fighting that took place at Nakijin on 3m 26d (30 April).

Shimazu Ryūkyū Gunseiki provides circumstantial evidence that a fierce attack on Nakijin happened. The first castle assaulted by the raiders in the account is referred to as Yōkeidan, where a battle takes place. In later elaborations of the story, a heroic Satsuma samurai called Hikita Jūza'emon is credited with smashing the gate down with a huge axe, a scene illustrated by a suitably dramatic picture in the illustrated *gunkimono*, *Ehon Ryūkyū Gunki*.

The neutralization of Nakijin, however it was brought about, allowed the Satsuma fleet undisputed use of Unten Harbour, and it was as they lay at anchor between Kourijima and the Motobu peninsula that the priest Kyan caught his first glimpse of the invasion force. From this point onwards Kyan's diary, the *Kyan Nikki*, provides a detailed account of the operation from the Ryūkyūan side. In spite of his obvious fears for the future, Kyan allowed himself a brief moment of admiration for the enemy fleet, splendidly bedecked as it was with long white and red *nobori* banners, *fukinuki* streamers and *uma jirushi*, all of which were being tossed about like flowers in the wind. This description, however, appears in the diary before Kyan's first dated reference to an event, which concerns the despatch of an envoy to Oshima on 3m 10d (14 April) as soon as news had been received of the Satsuma departure. This is certainly the incident noted above when ships bound for Oshima outran the Shimazu off Tokunoshima, and is one of the few events of the campaign to be recorded in the diaries of both Kyan and Ichiki.

The arrival of the invading army on Kourijima was not just noticed by Kyan. As the news spread southwards it caused panic among the population of Nakagami, the central area of Okinawa that was the old principality of Chūzan, and even the inhabitants of Naha Port were thrown into confusion. The events are recorded by Kyan in his diary:

When they heard that warships had arrived at Nakijin on the 16th day there was pandemonium throughout the whole country; with household goods being carried out to the four points of the compass; such things that I have never heard of happening before … from Naha, Tomari, Wakasachō, Kumemura and Izumizaki, various possessions were loaded on to horses or piled on to carts and blocked the roads. A multitude both high and low were in a state of chaos.

Kyan's diary then reveals that even at this late stage, three separate attempts were made to reach a negotiated settlement. The first was launched on 3m 27d (1 May) as the fleet lay at anchor in Unten Harbour and the Satsuma army was assaulting Nakijin Castle:

We rowed out to one of the enemy ships riding at anchor on the open sea to make contact. Five or six guns were already pointing out to the west of the ship ready to fire, as we beckoned with our war fans. It was like stroking the beard of a dragon or stamping on a tiger's tail.

Kyan and his bold colleagues were unable to talk to Kabayama Hisataka, who was directing the attack on Nakijin, and being told that no negotiations would be entertained, left empty-handed.

Even though Unten provided a safe haven, the decision was made to leave Kourijima behind as the Shimazu headquarters to which they could return, and to sail much further down the coast to another anchorage before splitting the army in two for the advance on Naha and Shuri. After securing Nakijin, the Shimazu re-embarked and sailed round the Motobu peninsula and down the coast to moor at Owan, where the ships were secured by hawsers. The precise location cannot be identified from the name but as Owan means 'the great bay', it was probably the sheltered harbour now called Yomitan that is located in a deep gulf about halfway between Motobu and Naha. An advance to Yomitan would illustrate the confidence the Shimazu had in their military superiority because, like Unten, Yomitan was also theoretically protected by fortifications. To the north lay the *gusuku* of Zakimi, while not much further away were the castles of Nakagusuku and Katsuren. Echoing what had happened at Nakijin, the Shimazu were not stopped by a *gusuku*. To attack their

General Kabayama Hisataka of the Shimazu army (named here as Tadahisa) treats with contempt the envoys from the king of Ryūkyū who have arrived with offers of negotiation. (ERGM)

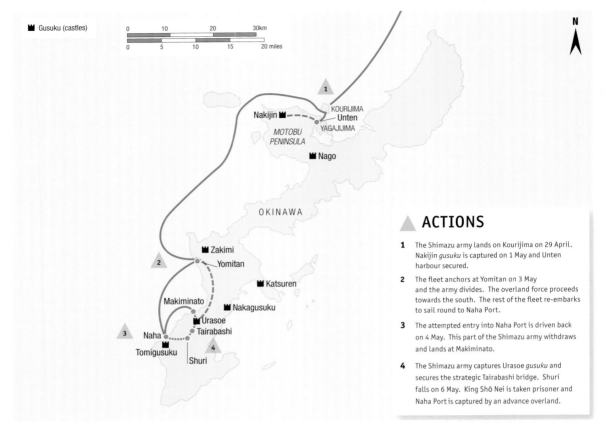

Gusuku (castles)

0   10   20   30km
0   5   10   15   20 miles

N

KOURIJIMA
Unten
Nakijin
YAGAJIJIMA
MOTOBU PENINSULA

Nago

OKINAWA

Zakimi
Yomitan

Katsuren

Makiminato
Nakagusuku

Urasoe
Tairabashi
Naha
Tomigusuku
Shuri

ACTIONS

1   The Shimazu army lands on Kourijima on 29 April. Nakijin *gusuku* is captured on 1 May and Unten harbour secured.

2   The fleet anchors at Yomitan on 3 May and the army divides. The overland force proceeds towards the south. The rest of the fleet re-embarks to sail round to Naha Port.

3   The attempted entry into Naha Port is driven back on 4 May. This part of the Shimazu army withdraws and lands at Makiminato.

4   The Shimazu army captures Urasoe *gusuku* and secures the strategic Tairabashi bridge. Shuri falls on 6 May. King Shō Nei is taken prisoner and Naha Port is captured by an advance overland.

The final phase of the raid from the landing on Kourijima to the surrender of Shuri.

28 APRIL 1609

Okinoerabujima surrenders

Shimazu assailants in the open, the garrisons of Nakagusuku and Katsuren would have had to abandon their fortified positions and not even a token sortie was mounted from nearby Zakimi.

At Yomitan, Kyan was involved in a further unsuccessful attempt to make contact with the invaders, but once again the bold envoys were rebuffed, and the weather simply added to their sense of approaching doom. The boat in which Kyan was travelling was forced to put in at the port of Makiminato near Urasoe Castle, from where he made a painful return to Shuri:

Lifting high the skirts of our *hakama*, we left Makiminato barefoot in a mad scramble. At that moment torrential rain starting falling; the blowing wind lifted up the sand, and the driving rain meant we could see nothing. We climbed over Esozan and other steep and dangerous places but endured this until we reached a flat area although we were very frightened. Blood from our feet stained the sand, and the skirts of our white *hakama* were crimson; when we looked back we saw that the houses beyond the beach had been burned to the ground. These villages were just the start. By midday it was as if nowhere on this island was not on fire. The sight of the people fleeing to the mountains through the storm was a strange one, like the leaves from trees in winter. We finally arrived at the guard post at Urasoe and for a moment gathered our breath; the people plied us with questions, but we had no answers for them. In the depths of the night we reached Shuri and entered the royal castle. We, the king's messengers, were dyed crimson, which provoked fear in the royal palace.

A view looking from the island of Kourijima back to the mainland of Okinawa, showing the area of sea where the Satsuma fleet anchored upon its arrival. Kourijima provided a base for the Shimazu army as it made its way by land and sea towards the capital.

The Advance Overland

The Satsuma army only stayed for a short time at Yomitan. The terror their initial arrival had caused, with the burning of buildings along the way, rapidly created the situation of chaos they had intended in order to render any defence more difficult. It was time to begin the major two-pronged assault. One half of the army would continue along the coast by ship and attack the harbour of Naha. The other half was to proceed overland and assault Shuri Castle. Accounts are given of the overland advance from the attacking and defending positions because both Ichiki Magobe'e Iemoto and Kyan were witnesses to it. Ichiki, in a characteristically brief description, writes:

> On the first day of the fourth month at the Hour of the Hare all the army on the overland route held a council of war. All the ships however, were of course at sea making us look like pair of outstretched hands. The council of war was held at Koanma.

'Koanma' has been identified as Kowan, a place within the modern metropolitan boundaries of Urasoe. The *gusuku* of Urasoe was the last fortification to be

29 APRIL 1609

Shimazu land on Kourijima off Okinawa Island

The harbour of Unten, sheltered from the sea by the islands of Kourijima and Yagajishima, is a safe natural anchorage, but was defended by the *gusuku* of Nakijin, so Nakijin became the first target on mainland Okinawa.

The natural harbour of Yomitan on the west coast of Okinawa. After securing Kourijima the Shimazu fleet re-embarked and landed half the army at Yomitan for the advance overland. The rest of the fleet then sailed down the coast to attack Naha Port.

encountered before Shuri, so the advance from Yomitan must have been rapid. Kyan provides brief details about the assault against Urasoe Castle, which includes the razing of the nearby Ryūfukuji Temple. Once again there is no detailed account of the attack on the castle itself, but it is likely that the tactic of sweeping the defenders off the walls using volleys of arquebus fire and breaking in the gates was used. This is certainly implied by Ichiki, who covers the entire advance from Yomitan to Shuri in a very brief statement that simply says: 'The *ashigaru-shū* attacked Shuri with firearms. Most importantly, we set fire to everything round about, and then the army converged on Shuri.' As he made his way from Makiminato to Urasoe, Kyan's observation of burning buildings is a reminder that the same tactic had been successfully used in 1592 during the initial Japanese blitzkrieg on Korea.

The next potential physical obstacle for the invading army was the Taiheikyō (Taihei Bridge) over a river on the road from Urasoe to Shuri, at the place now called Tairabashi. In 1597, King Shō Nei had ordered the wooden planked bridge to be replaced by one made of stone. Tairabashi continued to have strategic significance for many centuries, and during the battle of Okinawa in 1945, the Japanese army destroyed it to prevent the advance of US forces. Kyan describes its defence in 1609 as follows:

> When he heard of an enemy advance against Tairabashi, Goeku Ueekata set out as our general with over 100 men under him to defend the bridge. The enemy attacked the bridge in a hail of bullets. We did not know about guns like these; Gusukuma Sasu Peejin was wounded on the left side of his abdomen and then his head was taken. Seeing this, the men who remained retreated, and everyone sought security in the castle. All the houses in the vicinity were burned to the ground.

Once again the witness account describes a combination of firearms and fire. The strange title *peejin*, for the brave man who defended the bridge, refers to a local official with a local responsibility, not an inherited title, so the man described here was the officer responsible for Gusukuma, an area within Urasoe.

The Advance by Sea

With the capture of Urasoe and Tairabashi, the road to Shuri was open and the section of the Shimazu army that advanced by land was enjoying unqualified success. As for the assault by sea, neither Ichiki nor Kyan knew how the situation was progressing, but the author of *Ryūkyū Gunki* was a sea-captain, who actually made the short voyage down the west coast to Naha Port. Here the Shimazu encountered their only setback during the entire campaign because the diarist writes that at Naha, the Satsuma advance was temporarily stopped by the harbour defences. As noted earlier, these consisted of two stone castles with a chain between them and several cannon mounted in loopholes. Kabayama Hisataka's flagship wisely stayed out in the bay, while the sea-captain from the Seven Islands led the attack as follows:

> However, the harbour mouth of Naha was 25 *ken* wide, while round its inner waters over a length of 50 *ken* were high stone walls in which were loopholes where large cannon were mounted, and it was blocked by a net of iron stretched taut from the bottom of the harbour; the general Jana Ueekata with 3,000 men on the right hand side of the net fired cannon and completely frustrated the attack. One man was even wounded while out at sea, while General Kabayama's ship remained outside, because even the general's ship could not enter. The ships had to stay more than 5 *ri* out on the raging waves and could not attack.

The Ryūkyūan side heralded the repulse of the Shimazu from Naha as their great triumph of the campaign, but their success was to be very short-lived. For while all their defensive effort had been concentrated on preventing access to Naha Port, the rapid overland advance of the Satsuma army against Shuri was soon to make their Naha resistance redundant. Yet it may be the Shimazu retreat was not all that it seemed and the assault against Naha could have been merely a feint, designed to persuade the Ryūkyūan defenders to concentrate even more of their military resources around the harbour than was already the case. Such a strategy would have been completely in accordance with the way the Shimazu had conducted their campaigns for almost a century. In fact the use of a feint, or even a false retreat, had become something of a Satsuma trademark. A flying column would entice the enemy to attack and then withdraw in good order, so allowing the pursuing army to be surrounded. This tactic had worked successfully at the battles of Kisakihara in 1573, Mimigawa in 1578, Okita-Nawate in 1584 and Hetsugigawa in 1586. At the siege of Iwaya in 1586, a similar move had even allowed the Shimazu to entice their enemy into leaving the security of a fortress.

In the absence of any written account by the leader of the attack, Kabayama Hisataka, such a plan cannot be proved either way. What is known is that Kabayama rapidly abandoned any attempt to force his way into Naha Port and landed at least part of his army a short distance to the north, probably at Makiminato, the nearest

OVERLEAF

Two types of ships were used during the invasion: the heavy *ataka bune* (1), the standard warship of a *daimyo*'s navy, and the sleeker *sengoku bune* (2), normally a ship for carrying rice but here pressed into service for the invasion.

The most important elements of the defence of Naha Port on Okinawa were two forts at the harbour entrance. This depiction of Mie *gusuku* appears on a lacquered tray in the Reimeikan Museum in Kagoshima. It is copied from a painted screen showing Okinawa during the Edo Period. In the foreground is a boat bearing the flag of the Shimazu who controlled the islands following the action of 1609.

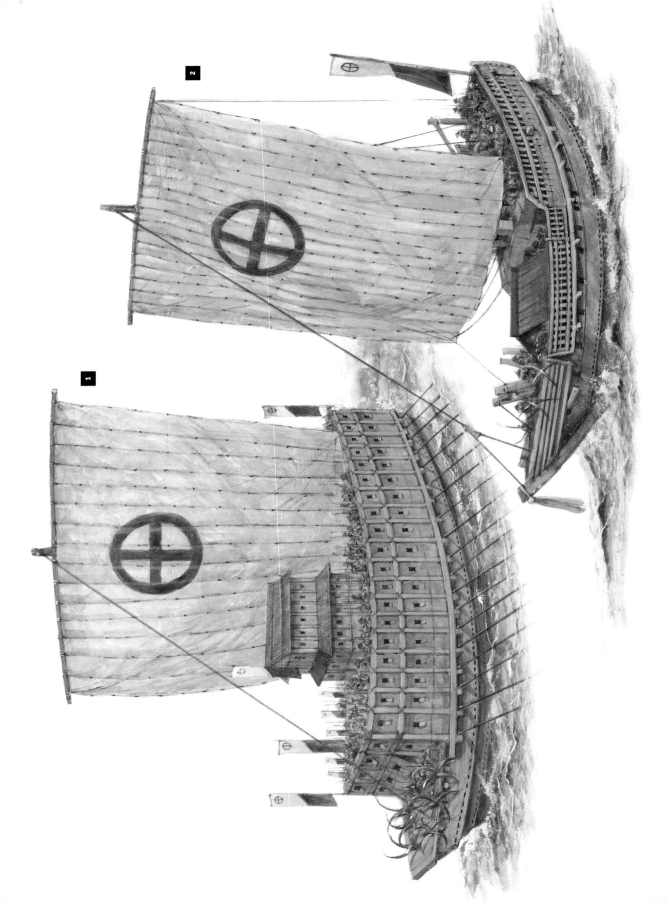

With its scale shown by the security man now guarding it, the Kyūkeimon (Gate of Long Happiness) shows the typical detail of one of the side gates of Shuri Castle. The low parapet without merlons or loopholes was very vulnerable to attack. As it is located on the northern side of the castle the Kyūkeimon would have been among the first parts of the castle to be attacked after the fall of Urasoe.

harbour to Urasoe. It appears that some of the Satsuma army stayed at sea, because there is record of them later making an unopposed entry into Naha after Shuri had fallen. Even if a deliberate feint had not formed part of his initial plan, Kabayama's decision to land and attack elsewhere shows good strategy skills. His decisions were no doubt facilitated by excellent intelligence, liaison and communication between the different units of the Satsuma army, a process that would have been carried out bravely and methodically by the highly mobile courier guards.

The account of the sea-captain suggests the Shimazu regarded the defeat at Naha as a minor setback in military terms, but an insult in the political context. He describes the atrocious conduct of the Shimazu samurai, who behaved as if avenging a great wrong when they landed further up the coast:

> They dragged their boats up and set them in place, then six samurai and 240 men from the Shichitō force went towards Naha. As it was the third month old and young, men and women, were gathered together weeding the wheat fields. When we caught sight of these people they were frightened and went and concealed themselves in the wheat

1 MAY 1609

Nakijin Castle occupied

The Kankaimon, the ironically named 'Gate of Welcome', was the first gate within the limestone walls of Shuri Castle to be attacked by the Shimazu after they had passed through the ornamental Shureimon. On either side stands a *shisha*, the 'lion dogs' that protect buildings on Okinawa from evil. Stubborn resistance was urged by a Ryūkyūan soldier from his post above the Kankaimon.

fields. [Kabayama] Mino-no-kami dono commanded Hikosaku, one of the *funegashira* of the Seven Islands, to go and capture them, and they were all killed. With my own sword, with which I had been presented some time ago, I cut down twelve or thirteen people and it was not at all damaged.

The Fall of Shuri Castle

Two armies were now converging on Shuri from the general direction of Urasoe, news of which soon reached the successful defenders of Naha. When they heard of the assault on Shuri, commanders Jana Teidō and Tomigusuku Seizoku hurriedly pulled troops out of Naha to defend the capital. It was, however, already too late. Kyan notes that a final attempt at negotiation with the advancing army was considered but rejected, because 'the houses were already burning'.

Shuri Castle was now isolated. Like Nakijin and the other castles, Shuri was a *gusuku* with the same characteristic limestone walls, gracefully curved and with exquisite masonry. However, where administrative buildings had been built within the inner baileys of Nakagusuku and Katsuren, Shuri boasted the palace of the kings of Ryūkyū. The fortress occupied a naturally strong position on a hill 130m above sea level at its highest point, giving a panoramic view across to Naha Port. Dating originally from the late 14th century, the castle was probably completed before 1427. Four decades later, Shuri had witnessed the coup d'état that toppled the first Shō dynasty and replaced it by the second Shō dynasty under King Shō En.

In a design similar to that of Nakijin, the approach to Shuri was covered by a number of gates. The first, the delicate Shureimon (Gate of Prosperity) on the western side, was purely ornamental. It was completed in about 1555. The main defensive western wall of Shuri extended to the Kankaimon, where an archway, above which a gatehouse had been built, cut through the defences. Stout doors filled the portal. On either side of the gate, spiritual protection was provided by a pair of *shisha*, one with its mouth open, the other with it closed, that would traditionally guard homes on Okinawa from evil spirits. Steps then rose up to the Zuisenmon (Great Auspicious Fountain Gate) and the Rōkokumon (Water Clock Gate). Here senior officials in the Ryūkyū court would dismount from their palanquins. The nearby Kōfukumon (Gate of Happiness) was a red wooden structure that was used as an administrative building. It led to the lower official courtyard in front of the similarly constructed Hōshinmon (Gate of Worship). This was the final gate before entering the inner palace courtyard called the *una*, which lay directly in front of the *seiden*, the main hall of the royal palace. Investitures and other major ceremonies of the kingdom of Ryūkyū were held in the open air in the *una*, which, together with the building surrounding it, resembled a miniature version of the Forbidden City of the Ming dynasty in Beijing, or the Gyeongbok Palace in Seoul of the kings of Korea, rather than any Japanese castle. The *seiden* itself was a three-storey building with a double-layered curved roof and decorated dragon pillars, and boasted lavish use of red and gold in vivid hues.

The walls of Shuri, even though they were as skilfully and as strongly built as those of the other *gusuku*, possessed no additional defences for the protection of their monarch. The outer sloping and smooth surfaces of the walls continued up to become parapets with no loopholes, behind which were simple flat walkways. Just as at Nakijin, their low elevation and modest slope made them an ideal target for an attack that combined firearms and scaling ladders. However, if persistent local tradition is to be believed, Shuri had a secret weapon. In preparation for the attack, the islanders had collected hundreds of *habu*, the large and deadly poisonous snakes that inhabited Ryūkyū, and had released them on the immediate approaches to the castle to lie in wait for the Satsuma army.

Kyan makes no reference to snakes in his diary. Instead, having described the brave attempt to hold back the enemy at Tairabashi and the widespread destruction of buildings by arson, he relates how the 'huge army' bore down upon the palace of Shuri:

> They soon gained control, and with Obu and Shōsei in the vanguard, the soldiers wearing different sorts of *yoroi* and different sorts of other armour, rushed up the walls like clouds that quickly gather and then as soon disappear; the [defending] soldiers set up two lines of wooden shields to the right and left of the pillars of the Shureimon Gate, but [the enemy] had already advanced as far as the lower gate.

An attempt was made to close the ornamental Shureimon using the large portable wooden shields that were common in Japanese warfare, but the Kyūkeimon on the northern side of the castle and the Kankaimon just above the Shūreimon were better places to hold back the attack. A brave and isolated act of defiance was witnessed by Kyan at the latter gate:

> At that moment, from on top of the tower on the Kankai Gate at the main entrance to Shuri, one single warrior urged total resistance, saying: 'The Satsuma rogues have come to attack us; but no matter how many there are, let's pick them off one by one!' In reality, such indiscreet words were the path to destruction. Not only the enemy but his allies heard it, and they despised him and warned him against it. With one man above and ten thousand below, it would have been better to do nothing, then nothing would happen; they said the man was possessed by a demon. The man was later taken prisoner.

A passage in *Kyūyō*, an official history of Ryūkyū compiled on Okinawa during the 18th century, relates a very similar incident. It describes a physician named Shuzō, who fought against the Shimazu in 1609. Like Kyan himself, this man was Japanese and was originally called Yamazaki Nikyū. He hailed from Echizen province, but fought on the side of his adopted country during the Satsuma raid:

> In 1609, when the Satsuma armies attacked our country, he defended the bell tower in the royal castle. When the Shimazu general's troops climbed upon the ramparts of the castle, Shuzō defended it with the utmost valour at the risk of his life. He pushed back the enemy. When, redoubling his efforts, Shuzō again made ready to defend the castle, our king, in his grief at his subjects' death in battle, decided to surrender. [Shuzō] withdrew from the castle, but while he was walking home, the Shimazu commander summoned him. The soldiers were delighted to arrest him.

Whether the two accounts describe the same man or not, the bravery of the gate defenders proved no more effective than the presence on either side of the portals of the stone *shisha*. Covered by successive hailstorms of bullets, the Satsuma samurai sprang up the scaling ladders and took command of Shuri's ramparts. The gates were smashed in, and soon terrified officials inside the castle were lowering themselves down by ropes from the most distant walls and fleeing, an incident noted by Ichiki Magobe'e Iemoto when he entered the palace.

In no time at all the vanguard of the Shimazu army was standing in the main courtyard outside the *seiden*. It would appear that throughout the attack, King Shō Nei had courageously remained at his post but, seeing that the cause was hopeless, he surrendered to avoid further bloodshed. His three *sanshikan*, Jana Teidō, Nago Ryōhō and Urasoe Chōshi, all of whom had fought bravely at Naha and Shuri, went voluntarily as hostages to the Shimazu to provide a guarantee of sincerity. As Shuri

THE SAMURAI FLEET APPROACHES NAHA HARBOUR
4 MAY 1609

One half of the Shimazu army proceeded overland from Yomitan while a direct assault was made on the harbour of Naha. This was defended by two fortresses between which an iron chain was strung, and with cannon mounted on the walls. By these means, the Shimazu fleet was prevented from entering the harbour and was forced to retreat and land the samurai further along the coast. Here we are looking towards the harbour entrance where the vanguard of the Shimazu fleet has been stopped by the chain and is coming under fire.

NAHA HARBOUR
DEFENCES 1 - 5

1 West Bay

2 Inner Harbour

3 The outlying harbour defences on the Nama no Ue promontory

4 Mie fortress

5 Yarazamori fortress

had fallen, making any remaining Ryūkyūan defence of Naha pointless, the Shimazu turned on Naha from the landward side. The inhabitants fled in such terror, their plight even touched Ichiki Magobe'e Iemoto:

> The land and sea divisions combined and the whole army then converged on Naha. The people of Ryūkyū were terrified, and the sight of them heading off in all directions towards the mountains is something my brush is incapable of describing; in the Naha area every house was abandoned. The entire army took over the dwellings within Naha. From the Takayama-shū, Ijuin Hisamoto took up residence in a two-storey building from where there was a view across the sea.

On 4m 3d (6 May), the king's belongings were carried out of the castle, and within 24 hours, King Shō Nei had been taken from Shuri in a palanquin as a prisoner of the Shimazu. His queen left on foot and took up temporary residence with her husband in the house of Nago Ryōhō, and to everyone's great unease, the king's son and heir also left the capital as a hostage. There was one final act of defiance when Urasoe Chōshi's three sons sought revenge for their father having been taken as a hostage. On that same day, 4m 4d (7 May), they slipped out of the castle in secret and attacked a number of Shimazu samurai at nearby Shikina, the summer palace of the Ryūkyūan kings. Two Shimazu officers are named as victims in the account:

> The fighting was fierce, and the clashing of their *tsuba* could have started a fire. Shōzonbō was struck dead. Hoga was wounded, but finally all three of the brothers were killed.

The following morning the Shimazu began the thorough and systematic process of looting Shuri Castle. For eight days they seized personal possessions and loaded them on to the Satsuma ships that had by now been able to make an unopposed entry into

BELOW
Hand-to-hand combat takes place during the attack on Shuri as a Satsuma samurai stabs his opponent with his *wakizashi*. (ERG)

OPPOSITE
A samurai retainer in the division commanded by Sano Masakata breaks into the palace of Shuri and cuts down a member of the royal family while terrified women look on. (ERG)

Naha. Ichiki Magobe'e Iemoto pays great attention to the plundering, and his own name appears in the list of those who took part. Among the treasures seized were priceless Buddhist scriptures that had come originally from Korea, along with treasures of gold, silver and lacquer. Apart from looting, the Satsuma samurai celebrated their victory in other ways, as the sea-captain refers in *Ryūkyū Gunki* to a three-day long *sake*-drinking bout. The area around Shuri, Naha and Urasoe was either deserted or burned to the ground, and the population, too terrified to return to their destroyed homes from the hills where they had concealed themselves, were now beginning to die from exhaustion and hunger.

Kabayama Hisataka had almost completed the task with which he had been entrusted by his lord. Hoping for a bloodless conquest of the islands of Kumejima and Miyakojima, he despatched the *sanshikan* by ship to inform the inhabitants of what had happened and to demand their surrender. The scheme succeeded, and by 5m 5d (6 June) the outer islands had submitted to Satsuma rule without even seeing an invader. Prior to this, however, important steps had been taken to secure the island of Okinawa. Honda Chikamasa and Kamaike Yoshiemon were ordered to stay behind in Naha with a number of soldiers as an occupying garrison. The remainder of the victorious Satsuma army set sail for home with Shō Nei, the king of Ryūkyū, as their prisoner and prize. Kyan sailed with his king, and at Kourijima, within sight of Nakijin, he wrote the following passage:

In past times we would dance with joy at the glory of the flowers of the summer, but in this present year of Keichō they have been transformed into the grass of autumn. Those who are born are certain to perish. Happiness has ended and sorrow has come like a farewell note from ancient times. At this moment in time, while we are being besieged in our homes as if we were in prison, and the women and children of our families have run to the four points of the compass trying to escape, on mountain and field the number of bodies is increasing.

OVERLEAF
The 'secret weapon' employed by the defenders of Shuri, the royal palace and castle of the king of Ryūkyū, was to let loose hundreds of the deadly *habu*, the poisonous snakes native to Okinawa. Although there are no records of the Shimazu army being stopped by the *habu*, this plate shows the scene that may well have occurred. We are standing at the west side of Shuri were the first line of defence is the Shureimon, a ceremonial gate made of wood, defended against the Shimazu by a simple shieldwall. The approaching samurai have come under attack from the snakes.

The fleet suffered a difficult and stormy crossing via the Amami Islands to Satsuma, but on 4m 25d (28 May) the Shimazu army, with Kabayama Hisataka at its head, made a triumphant return to Kagoshima with their task successfully completed and, uniquely in Japanese history, with a captured foreign monarch in tow. The king was paraded honourably enough in front of the grandees of the Shimazu court, in a rehearsal for the ordeal that awaited him when he was to be taken to meet the Tokugawa *shogun*.

The Satsuma objectives had been achieved for a modest casualty list of between 100 and 200 men during the course of the entire operation. Two individual names appear in a document in the Kagoshima collection; both would appear to relate to the final act of defiance mounted by the sons of Urasoe Chōshi:

4th month, 2nd day
Umekita Shōzonbō: crossed over to Ryūkyū and at the time of the fall of Shuri died in action in the hard fighting, as did the name below:
Komatsu Hikokurō: *funegashira* of the Seven Islands, died in action at Shikina.

The Ryūkyūan sources note that deaths occurred on Tokunoshima, but apart from the loss of 500 men who tried to stop the advance from Nakijin, this appears to be the only figure available for Ryūkyūan casualties in the whole campaign.

A King's Ransom

King Shō Nei remained a hostage of the Shimazu until 1611, during which time he was taken by Shimazu Iehisa to Sumpu (Shizuoka) to meet Tokugawa Ieyasu and to Edo to meet the *shogun*, Tokugawa Hidetada. The long journey is minutely described by Kyan, who lists every stopping place, the distance between towns and the daily weather along the way. There are moments of poetry, but also of great sadness, because the king's brother was taken ill at Sumpu:

Prince Shō Kō succumbed to a serious illness, which caused us great sadness, so prayers were offered in every temple and shrine and the techniques of *yin* and *yang* performed, doctors prescribed medicine, but to no avail.

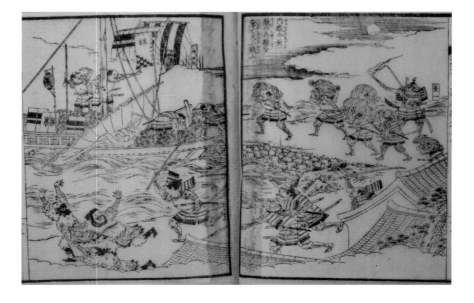

The victorious Satsuma army plunder the palace of Shuri in the aftermath of their successful raid. In the foreground we see the ordinary inhabitants of Okinawa being chased away at swordpoint. Vast quantities of treasure were carried off to Kagoshima when Shuri was captured. (ERG)

The prince became too ill to travel, and much later in their journey Kyan records the sad news of his death.

Tokugawa Ieyasu had already written to Shimazu Iehisa to formally present him with Ryūkyū as his reward, and numerous gifts followed. Shō Nei did not return to his kingdom until certain plans were well in hand: a census of population and resources, a scheme for the Satsuma administration of Ryūkyū, the re-drawing of borders and the humiliation of the royal family. The surrender oath began with the words noted earlier that referred to the status of Ryūkyū as a feudal dependency of Satsuma since ancient times. That no such relationship had ever been exercised, even if it had existed on paper, exposed the whole device as a cynical rewriting of history. Expressions of overflowing gratitude towards the Shimazu, who had chastised the Ryūkyūans for their waywardness and then mercifully allowed their king to return, added to the pantomime. Only one senior official refused to agree to the package of lies: Jana Teidō, who had bravely led the defence of the port of Naha, was taken to one side and beheaded, and no other member of the *sanshikan* dared follow his lead.

At first, the submission of Ryūkyū to the Shimazu, and thereby to the Tokugawa, had been a prize of war. This situation rapidly moved to being a one-way peace process. Throughout the year 1610 Satsuma *bugyō*, who acted as commissioners in wartime and magistrates in peacetime, carried out a thorough survey of all the land on the Ryūkyū Islands to assess their value in *koku*. To the Shimazu, who had just undergone a similar process when they had been beaten by Toyotomi Hideyoshi in 1587, this was merely an administrative exercise that the Ryūkyūans had avoided for many years. They applied themselves to the task with vigour, employing a total of 168 staff. But to the losing side this was a further humiliation, particularly when all the Amami Islands were excluded from the valuation and were incorporated into the Satsuma *han* in 1611.

King Shō Nei was allowed to return to Okinawa only after putting his seal on the document that had cost Jana Teidō his life. Apart from agreeing to the fictitious statement that Ryūkyū had always been a feudal dependency of Satsuma, the king was forced to swear that it was his own disrespect for the *shogun* that had brought the situation about. As a further insult, he also had to agree that it was only through

King Shō Nei of Ryūkyū is made to sign the surrender document by the triumphant Shimazu general. The artist has endeavoured to show that the scene is taking place within the precincts of the royal palace at Shuri. (ERG)

The beautifully restored Seiden or Main Hall of the royal palace of Shuri, where the architecture is like that of the Forbidden City in Beijing. Here King Shō Nei remained at his post until he realized that his cause was lost and surrendered to the Shimazu army to prevent further bloodshed.

3 MAY 1609

Fleet anchors at Yomitan; army divides

the generosity of Shimazu Iehisa that he was being permitted to return. The king's ransom was never expressed in monetary terms; instead it was paid in kind, through the complete surrender of his sovereignty in all but name. He lived for another nine years, and as death approached, he was overwhelmed by a sense of failure and guilt. He therefore decreed that he was not worthy to be laid to rest in the great tomb of Tamaudun where all the kings of his dynasty were buried. Instead he was interred in a modest tomb in the hillside below Urasoe castle, and a mask was placed upon his face.

Ashamed at his failure to resist the conquest of his kingdom by the *daimyo* of Satsuma, King Shō Nei of Ryūkyū decreed that when he died he should not be buried in the tomb of his ancestors beneath the castle of Shuri, but here at Urasoe, in a cliff beneath Urasoe *gusuku*, the fortress that was the last defence before Shuri.

ANALYSIS

As the embers cooled from the remains of Shuri Castle, both sides began to analyse the means by which the Shimazu had been so successful and why the kingdom of Ryūkyū had allowed itself to be so thoroughly humiliated. It was from these considerations that a number of myths developed about the effectiveness of the Satsuma operation, and the culpability of certain Ryūkyūan officials involved in the defence of the realm who were to be cast in the role of scapegoat.

From the victorious Satsuma side there was a clear recognition that the raid had been well planned. Not only had numbers and weapons been carefully chosen and coordinated, but the operation had been carried out with speed and great efficiency. Tactically, the campaign drew upon the experience of the similar situation in 1592 which had highlighted the difficulties of a sea assault against land defended by castles. Yet it had not been totally straightforward for the Shimazu because as *Ryūkyū Gunki* reveals, only the island of Okinoerabujima surrendered meekly. Resistance on Amami-Oshima, Tokunoshima and Okinawa itself was fierce, but it was the Shimazu superiority in firearms, and their readiness to use both fire and sword in a ruthless manner against soldiers and non-combatants alike, that finally decided the matter.

With such a clear-cut victory it may be thought that a simple and factual account of the triumph, whereby an army only 3,000 strong had captured a kingdom, would have sufficed as a historical record. Nevertheless, for reasons that probably have more to do with samurai mythology than political reality, the Shimazu produced a written account of the operation that implied, among other falsehoods, that the raid involved 100,000 men. This was the *gunkimono* known as *Shimazu Ryūkyū Gunseiki*, compiled in 1663, in which the whole operation was turned into a heroic military romance. Two centuries later the text of *Shimazu Ryūkyū Gunseiki* formed the basis for an illustrated version called *Ehon Ryūkyū Gunki*. This contained dramatic woodblock pictures by Hokkyō Okada Gyokuzan (1737–1812), who had previously illustrated *Ehon Taikōki*, a fictionalized life of Hideyoshi, from which he reproduced several pictures. In *Ehon Ryūkyū Gunki* the stories of samurai exploits receive further elaboration. In 1868 the book was republished in one volume using metal type, using new illustrations by Ogata Gekko (1859–1920).

4 MAY 1609

Fleet repulsed from Naha Port

5 MAY 1609

Armies converge on Shuri

The Name no Ue Shrine occupies a position on a dramatic cliff to the north of Naha Port. The site provided a vantage point during the Shimazu army's attack on the harbour in 1609, and now houses a memorial to Jana Teidō, the brave general who led the defence of Naha.

The Scapegoat

On the Ryūkyūan side, the kingdom's rulers were keen to demonstrate that it had not been their fault such a calamity had overtaken them, and the most noble victim of this scapegoat attitude was Jana Teidō. As already noted, he was a member of the *sanshikan* whose son-in-law had tried to defend Tokunoshima. His own role during the invasion was to defend Naha Port, which he did very successfully, and Jana Teidō only withdrew to Shuri Castle when he realised how the overall attack was developing. There is no argument over his behaviour in battle, nor is there any dispute over his heroism when he refused to sign the humiliating surrender document and paid with his life. Yet it was Jana Teidō who was cast in the role of villain, who alone was said to have brought disaster on the kingdom. This judgement comes originally from Kyan, who twice mentions Jana Teidō's supposed guilt in his diary. First, before describing the invasion, he states: 'Jana when young, went to Nanjing in the Great Ming, and because of a long stay there, did not understand Japanese ways and thus helped bring about a disaster.' Then, almost at the end of his account, he writes: 'If one looks for the cause of Ryūkyū's present woes, it is the fault of one person, Jana Teidō.' Two sentences later he adds, almost as an afterthought: 'I now hear that he has been beheaded.'

It was an accusation that was to be repeated in the years to come, when Ryūkyūan scholars under the influence of their Satsuma overlords heaped calumny upon the 'evil' Jana Teidō. They charged him with failing to recognize the benevolence of Shimazu rule and the benefits that would have flowed had such hegemony been exercised without the inconvenience of a war. This was, of course, exactly what the Satsuma overlords wanted to hear, and this judgement has been accepted without question by certain modern writers on the topic. Matsuda writes:

> He miscalculated the changing conditions of the time, and this led to the invasion of the island by Satsuma troops. He was finally taken prisoner and executed in Kagoshima... Teidō was ignorant of the trend of the times and defied the summons of the lord of Satsuma for submission... The impasse in negotiations between Ryūkyū and Satsuma could not be undone because of his strong stand. He alone was to blame.

Whether Jana Teidō deserves such a devastating posthumous condemnation is debatable as it is not known whether he was ever in a position to have actually influenced the situation. When he was appointed to the *sanshikan* in 1605, the Shimazu had long had a claim to Ryūkyū, and had been making plans since the time of Hideyoshi. Furthermore, as the trigger for action was actually the decision made by the *shogun* many hundreds of miles away, an official in the kingdom could hardly be accused of bringing about the confrontation. Today in Okinawa, Jana Teidō's rehabilitation appears to be complete, and a monument to him as a patriot stands in the park behind the Nami no Ue Shrine, which overlooks the harbour he defended so well in Naha.

The Peaceful Kingdom

Blame for the disaster was also laid against the former king of Ryūkyū, Shō Shin (1427–1506) who, according to popular myth, had caused Okinawa to be disarmed and thus left future generations defenceless. The myth of Ryūkyūan disarmament is no older than the early 19th century but is very persistent, and is particularly popular among the practitioners of *karate*. The premise for the story is that the peace-loving King Shō Shin arranged for all the weapons on Okinawa to be rounded up and stored away securely to prevent disorder in the kingdom. This resulted in a land of peace that was favourably remarked upon by many visitors. Unfortunately, when the Shimazu invaded there could be no armed resistance, so the Satsuma raid met with no opposition. The positive spin-off was that as the farmers needed to defend themselves from bandits and raiders, they could only use their bare fists or cunningly modified agricultural tools; and this, so the story goes, proved to be the foundation for karate and *nunchaku*.

The myth of pacifist Ryūkyū developed from travellers' tales of the early 19th century, when visitors to Ryūkyū described the islands as a haven of peace and tranquillity. One very influential enthusiast for this view was Captain Basil Hall, who visited Naha in 1816 with two British ships HMS *Lyra* and HMS *Alceste*. His observations were unlikely to have been so widely reported had he not made the island of St Helena a later port of call. Here he passed on his impressions of Ryūkyū to the exiled Napoleon Bonaparte who was amazed that a nation without arms, to whom war was unknown, could possibly exist. To a very large extent Hall's observations were accurate, but as foreign visitors were confined to a small geographical area, they were limited. He could not be expected to have seen either the few ceremonial weapons then available to the Ryūkyūans or any evidence of the far-from-pacific treatment meted out to offenders of Ryūkyū's harsh penal codes.

Another aspect of the militaristic side of Ryūkyūan life that Captain Hall would certainly not have seen were the swords worn by the swaggering Satsuma samurai based on Okinawa. Even though the Satsuma controlled the islands, they took great pains to ensure nobody knew about it, and invariably made themselves scarce when foreign visitors or traders arrived. This extraordinary behaviour was closely tied up with the role Ryūkyū had played in Japan's trade with China from 1609 onwards. For many centuries, trade and commerce with China had been carried out through a time-honoured deceit, whereby foreign nations were forced to go through the motions of paying tribute to the Chinese emperor. In return for these lavish displays of pretend acquiescence, the Imperial Son of Heaven would acknowledge the subservient kings as the rulers of their own countries, and all the benefits of trade would follow. Unlike Japan, which had always been reluctant to go through this pantomime, the kings of Ryūkyū had carried out tribute trade with China for many years prior to the Satsuma takeover.

By the mid-17th century, trade between China and Japan had become greatly restricted. For the Japanese, the policy of seclusion confined Chinese commercial interests to the port of Nagasaki, whilst the Chinese had to contend with the plundering *wakō*. But there was a loophole, and it was one exploited to the full by Satsuma, whereby the tribute trade with Ryūkyū was continued. Satsuma thereby acquired Chinese goods, which it sold at a vast profit to the rest of Japan.

For the surrogate Japanese tribute trade to succeed, the Chinese had to be prevented from discovering who was really in charge of Ryūkyūan affairs. In efforts to ensure the system would not be discontinued, elaborate steps were taken when Chinese traders arrived. Anything that displayed a Japanese name, such as a book, was hidden and the Japanese language and singing of Japanese songs could not be heard. If a Satsuma man was spoken to in Japanese by a Chinese official, he had to pretend that he did not understand. When Chinese envoys, who were likely to be better educated and more inquisitive than mere traders, arrived at Naha, even more stringent precautions were taken, and all Satsuma officials went by ship to a pre-arranged secret destination where they would wait until the Chinese departed.

It was the naive observations of foreign travellers, disguising reality, that sustained the myth of bare-fisted Okinawan warriors taking on armed Satsuma samurai. Yet the belief that Shō Shin had disarmed Ryūkyū was to be supported many years later by an idiosyncratic interpretation of an inscription on a monument erected in 1509

6 MAY 1609

Shuri Castle falls

at Urasoe, extolling the achievements of the king during his long reign. In 1932, Ifa Fuyu, the father of Okinawan studies, deciphered the fourth accomplishment listed there as meaning 'armour was used to make utensils'. Other readings, however, simply state that the king collected all the weapons and put them into a central store from which they could be drawn in times of emergency. As a parallel, weapons were confiscated in Hideyoshi's Sword Hunt of 1588, when the people were told their blades and guns would to be melted down to make bolts for a giant image of the Buddha that Hideyoshi was erecting in Kyoto. No-one claimed Hideyoshi was disarming Japan, but that he was merely disarming any potential opponents. There is no doubt that Shō Shin had a very similar aim.

Kerr, in his *Okinawa: A History of an Island People* notes a further similarity between Shō Shin's control of his powerful warlords and the requirement of the *shogun*, Iemitsu, that all *daimyo* should reside in Edo. Yet there is certainly no evidence that Shō Shin, his predecessors or his successors believed pacifism should be a national policy. In fact the history of Ryūkyū's aggressive expansion into the Yaeyama Islands and the Amami Islands along with earlier activities, would indicate the opposite. During the 15th century, Ryūkyū under Shō Toku was at the forefront of military innovation, particularly in the field of firearms. Their weapons may only have been primitive Chinese handguns, but as the Japanese had no firearms at all, the guns of a Ryūkyūan envoy were sufficient to amaze his hosts when he fired one during a visit to the *shogun* in 1466. It was the first gunpowder explosion heard in Japan since the attempted Mongol Invasions of 1274 and 1281.

Half a century later, far from disarming his country, the 'pacifist' King Shō Shin brought about the improvements in the defences of Naha that saved Ryūkyū from the *wakō* and stopped the seaborne wing of the Satsuma raid in 1609. However, compared with their development of large cannon, the Ryūkyūan kings had neglected the advance of the European-style arquebus, a weakness they shared with Korea. It is tempting to speculate what might have happened if the Ryūkyūan expansion northwards had gone just that little bit further in the 1500s and had taken in Tanegashima. The Portuguese traders of 1543 would then have landed in the territory of a king who already knew the potential of firearms.

A procession through the streets of Shuri by an official of the occupying Satsuma forces in the years after 1609 is shown here on a painted screen in Okinawa Prefectural Museum. The swords worn by the swaggering Satsuma samurai are clearly depicted. When Chinese envoys arrived on Okinawa the Satsuma rulers would make themselves scarce so that the Chinese did not know that Okinawa was occupied by Japan.

CONCLUSION

In conclusion, the Shimazu invasion of Ryūkyū was an operation carried out against a kingdom that was the equal of Satsuma in terms of bravery, and superior to it in terms of large-calibre artillery. Unfortunately for King Shō Nei, the brave men and the heavy guns were concentrated in the harbour area or on the very vulnerable walls of the *gusuku*, which were swept by concentrated arquebus fire under the cover of burning buildings. It was a crushing victory, and only the Ryūkyūan side felt any need to explain it away by treachery or ancient neglect.

From a military point of view the operation was a brilliant success. There are strong parallels with the invasion of Korea that had witnessed a seaborne landing, the successful deployment of massed firearms and the use of fire to create panic and confusion. But whereas the Korean campaign became bogged down at the Imjin River after a fierce initial advance, thereby letting the king of Korea escape, the rapid progress down Okinawa resulted in its king being captured and taken hostage. In other similarities with the Korean campaign, all three diarists note the horrific and cynical treatment of civilians whose terror was used as a weapon of war. The 1609 Okinawa raid involved strategy and tactics that drew on experiences from a century of successful samurai warfare and applied their lessons to great effect. However, it was a pattern never to be repeated. The two remaining samurai wars (Osaka and the Shimabara Rebellion) were to involve long sieges using artillery and, in the case of Osaka, a massive pitched battle. Okinawa 1609 was the last flourish of the highly mobile and seemingly disorganised pattern of warfare that reflected so well the individualistic behaviour of samurai ancestors. So strong was this tradition that it would be this aspect that would be stressed over and above the methodical strategic aspects when the Shimazu retainers eventually read about it in the *gunkimono*.

As to the final outcome, it is perhaps somewhat misleading to look upon the Shimazu as the victors and the Ryūkyūans as the losers. In terms of the overall Tokugawa hegemony, both were victims. The Shimazu had been conquered by the Tokugawa fewer than ten years before they were commanded to conquer Okinawa on their overlord's behalf. Just like the king of Ryūkyū, the Satsuma *daimyo* had been reinvested with his own territory in return for a pledge of loyalty, a supply of labour and tribute to the Tokugawa. The king of Ryūkyū, as the sovereign of an independent kingdom, may have suffered a greater fall than the Shimazu, who had been through the process twice, but the level to which the king fell was no lower.

▼

7 MAY 1609

King Shō Nei is taken prisoner

▼

28 MAY 1609

Shō Nei is paraded through Kagoshima

▼

Bowing low before his master, Shimazu Iehisa receives the congratulations of the *shogun* Tokugawa Hidetada following the successful completion of his mission to pacify the kingdom of Ryūkyū. (ERGM)

59

GLOSSARY

aji	hereditary warlords of Ryūkyū
ashigaru	foot soldiers
ataka bune	naval troop transports and warships
bugashira	subordinate general
bugyō	commissioners in wartime, magistrates in peacetime
daimyo	feudal lord
fudai daimyo	hereditary retainers of the Tokugawa
fukinuki	slashed cylindrical streamers
fune bugyō	ship commissioner
funegashira	ship's captain
gunkimono	war tale
gusuku	Okinawan term for castle or fortress
habu	poisonous breed of snakes
Hachiman	the god of war
han	territory held by a *daimyo*
haramaki	type of body armour, open at the back
hatamoto	'under the standard' – in effect the guards division
horo	stiffened cloaks worn by messengers on battlefields
ikusa metsuke	army superintendents
ishibiya	type of cannon
jinbaori	sleeveless surcoat
jingasa	samurai hat
kanme	unit of mass, equivalent to 3.75kg
katana	classic samurai sword
ken	unit of length, equivalent to 1.8m
ki	the counting suffix for horsemen that included a samurai's personal followers
ko uma jirushi	lesser battle-standard
koku	unit of measurement, being approx 180 litres of rice
kumade	'bear-paw' rake
kumi	group or unit
kumigashira	'captains' who commanded groups of men
kuwa	sickle blades mounted on long shafts
merlons	the solid part of a crenellated parapet
metsuke	censors and intelligence gatherers
mon	heraldic crest or badge; also gate
monogashira	'captains' who commanded groups of men
nagae-yari	long shafted spear
naginata	bladed weapon with a long shaft
nobori	long banners
nodachi	extra-long sword with very strong, long handle
nunchaku	twin-joined fighting sticks, sometimes called chain sticks
o uma jirushi	great battle-standard
prefecture	the office or area of authority
ri	unit of length equivalent to 3,927m
sake	alcoholic drink
sanseong	Korean term for mountain fortress
sanshikan	government body of the kingdom of Ryūkyū, commonly

	known as the "Council of Three"
sashimono	identifying banner or flag worn on the back
seppuku	ritual suicide by disembowelment, commonly known as *hara-kiri*
sengoku bune	large ships, widely used to transport goods
Sengoku jidai	time of conflict known as the 'Age of Warring States' from mid-15th to early 17th century
shisha	ornamental lion dogs thought to give spiritual direction
shogun	hereditary commander of the Japanese army
shogunate	the government, rule or office of a *shogun*
sonae	army unit
sōtaishō	commander-in-chief
taishō	subordinate general
tantō	dagger
tozama daimyo	'outer lords'; *daimyo* who had opposed Tokugawa
tsuba	sword guards
tsukai-ban	courier guards
uma jirushi	battle standard, literally 'horse insignia'
wakizashi	short sword, companion of the *katana*
wakō	Japanese pirates
yari	spear
yin and *yang*	complementary principles of Chinese philosophy
yoroi	armour
zori tori	sandal bearer

A Shimazu samurai kills a Ryūkyūan mounted warrior by dragging him down with one hand holding the man's spear as he thrusts at him with his own weapon. (ERGM)

FURTHER READING

Primary sources in Japanese

Diaries and *Gunkimono*

Kyan nikki [The Diary of Kyan Ueekata], *Naha-shi shi: shiryō hen 1 (2)* (Kumamoto, 1970) pp. 39–59

Ryūkyū tokai nichi ki [The Diary of Ichiki Magobe'e], *Naha-shi shi: shiryō hen 1 (2)* (Kumamoto, 1970) pp. 31–36, and also as Document 557 in *Kagoshima-ken shiryō: kyūki zatsuroku kohen 4*, (Kagoshima, 1983) pp. 212–216

Ryūkyū Gunki, Ryūkyū iri no ki, Document 659 in *Kagoshima-ken shiryō: kyūki zatsuroku kohen 4*, (Kagoshima, 1983) pp. 257–261; and in the following

Satsuryū Gundan Yamashita, Fumitake *Ryūkyū Gunki – Satsuryū Gundan (Amami-Ryūkyū Rekishi Shiryō Series 1)* (Kagoshima, 2007)

Shimazu Ryūkyū Gunseiki, Nakane Tomio (ed.), *Shimazu Ryūkyū Gunseiki* (Kōnosu-shi, Saitama-ken, 1995)

Illustrated books

Okada Gyokusan (illustrator), *Ehon Ryūkyū Gunki* (20 volumes) (Osaka, 1836–64)

Ogata Gekko (illustrator), *Ehon Ryūkyū Gunki Mokuroku* (Edo, 1868)

Secondary sources in Japanese

General

Kamiya, Nobuyuki, 'Satsuma Ryūkyū shinnyū', *Shin Ryūkyū shi, kinsei hen*, Vol. jō (Naha, 1989) pp. 33–72

Kamiya, Nobuyuki, 'Shimazu-ke no Ryūkyū shuppei to kenryoku hensei', *Okinawa shiryō henshūjo kiyō 5* (Naha, 1980) pp. 1–41

Takara, Kurayoshi, *Ryūkyū Okoku* (Tokyo, 1993) pp. 68–75

Wataguchi, Masakiyo, 'Jūnana seiki Satsuma no shinkō – sono gen-in ni tsuite', *Okinawa Rekishi Kenkyū 2* (1966) pp. 18–35

Military background to Okinawa

Toma, Shiichi, 'Hiya ni tsuite', *Nantō Koko* 14 (Dec. 1994) pp. 123–152

Uezato, Takashi, 'Ko-Ryūkyū no guntai to sono rekishiteki tenkai', *Ryūkyū Ajia shakai bunka kenkyūkai kiyō 5* (2002) pp. 105–128

Uezato, Takashi, 'Ryūkyū no kaki ni tsuite', *Okinawa Bunka 36* (2000) pp. 73–92

An evening view of the stone pavement of the old military road built in 1522 by King Shō Shin to link Naha Port with Shuri Castle.

Secondary sources in European languages

Binkenstein, R., 'Die Ryukyu-Expedition unter Shimazu Iehisa', *Monumenta Nipponica*, Vol. 4 (1941) pp. 622–628

Kerr, George H., *Okinawa: The History of an Island People (Revised Edition)*, afterword by Mitsugu Sakihara (North Clarendon VT, 2000)

Matsuda, Mitsugu, *The Government of the Kingdom of Ryukyu 1609–1872* (Unpublished PhD, Honolulu, 1967)

Matsuda, Mitsugu, 'The Ryukyuan Government Scholarship Students to China 1392–1868. Based on a short essay by Nakahara Zenchu, 1962', *Monumenta Nipponica*, Vol. 21 (1966) p. 293

Nelson, Thomas, 'Japan in the Life of Early Ryūkyū', *The Journal of Japanese Studies*, Vol. 32 (2006) pp. 367–392

Smits, Gregory, 'Romantic Ryukyu in Okinawan Politics: The Myth of Ryukyuan Pacifism', paper presented to the Association for Asian Studies Conference (San Francisco, February 2006)

Smits, Gregory, *Visions of Ryūkyū: Identity and Ideology in Early-Modern Thought and Politics* (Honolulu, 1999)

Toby, Ronald P., *State and Diplomacy in Early Modern Japan: Asia in the Development of the Tokugawa Bakufu* (Stanford University Press, 1991)

INDEX

References to illustrations are shown in **bold**.